TEXT AND PERFORMANCE

General Editor: Michael Scott

The series is designed to introduce sixth-form and under-graduate students to the themes, continuing vitality and performance of major dramatic works. The attention given to production aspects is an element of special importance, responding to the invigoration given to literary study by the work of leading contemporary critics.

The prime aim is to present each play as a vital experience in the mind of the reader – achieved by analysis of the text in relation to its themes and theatricality. Emphasis is accordingly placed on the relevance of the work to the modern reader and the world of today. At the same time, traditional views are presented and appraised, forming the basis from which a creative response to the text can develop.

In each volume, Part One: *Text* discusses key themes or problems, the reader being encouraged to gain a stronger perception both of the inherent character of the work and also of variations in interpreting it. Part Two: *Performance* examines the ways in which these themes or problems have been handled in modern productions, and the approaches and techniques employed to enhance the play's accessibility to modern audiences.

A synopsis of the play is given and an outline of its major sources, and a concluding Reading List offers guidance to the student's independent study of the work.

PUBLISHED

A Midsummer Night's Dream	Roger Warren
Antony and Cleopatra	Michael Scott
Hamlet	Peter Davison
Henry the Fourth, Parts 1 and 2	T. F. Wharton
King Lear	Gāmini Salgādo
Macbeth	Gordon Williams
Othello	Martin L. Wine
The Tempest	David L. Hirst
Twelfth Night	Lois Potter
Doctor Faustus	William Tydeman
Volpone	Arnold P. Hinchliffe

IN PREPARATION

Measure for Measure	Graham Nicholls
The Winter's Tale	R. P. Draper

OTHELLO

Text and Performance

MARTIN L. WINE

MACMILLAN

First published 1984

Published by
Higher and Further Education Division
MACMILLAN PUBLISHERS LTD
Houndmills, Basingstoke, Hampshire RG21 2XS
and London
Companies and representatives
throughout the world

Typeset by
Wessex Typesetters Ltd
Frome, Somerset

Printed in Hong Kong

British Library Cataloguing in Publication Data
Wine, Martin L.
Othello.–(Text and performance)
1. Shakespeare, William. Othello
I. Title   II. Series
822.3′3   PR2829
ISBN 0–333–34001–9

CONTENTS

Acknowledgements   6
General Editor's Preface   7
Plot Synopsis and Source   8

PART ONE: TEXT

1	Introduction	9
2	Structure as Meaning	20
3	Language as Action	29
4	Analysis of Speeches	36

PART TWO: PERFORMANCE

5	Introduction	42
6	Varieties of Theatrical Interpretation, 1943–82	43
7	Othello	45
8	Iago	57
9	Desdemona	66
10	Epilogue	73

Reading List   81
Index of Names   83

Illustrations appear in Part Two

6

ACKNOWLEDGEMENTS

Quotations of the text of the play are from the New Penguin
Shakespeare edition (1968), edited by Kenneth Muir.

I wish to thank Lawrence A. Bertrand for supplying me with an
advance copy of his book on televised Shakespeare (*Shakespeare's Vision: Verbal and Visual*) and Lawrence S. Poston, the
former head of my department, for providing time for research
and writing.

For making research such a pleasure I am grateful to the
following institutions and their staffs: the Performing Arts
Center of the New York Public Library and Museum of the
Performing Arts at Lincoln Center, New York; the Shakespeare
Centre Library, Stratford-upon-Avon; the Theatre Museum
(Victoria and Albert Museum, London); the Shakespeare
Production Office of bbc-television, London; the Public Play-
back Service of the British Institute of Recorded Sound,
London; Seymour Kravitz and Company, Publicity (New
York), and the Research Board of the University of Illinois at
Chicago.

Throughout the preparation of this volume I have benefited
from the conversation and insights of friends, colleagues and
students too numerous to mention here. I hope that all of them
are aware of how grateful I am. I must, however, single out
Professor Allan Casson, whose course in Shakespeare is
reputed to be one of the crown jewels in the curriculum of the
University of Southern California. The General Editor of the
series, Michael Scott, has been unfailingly helpful.

FOR

MY MOTHER

GENERAL EDITOR'S PREFACE

For many years a mutual suspicion existed between the theatre director and the literary critic of drama. Although in the first half of the century there were important exceptions, such was the rule. A radical change of attitude, however, has taken place over the last thirty years. Critics and directors now increasingly recognise the significance of each other's work and acknowledge their growing awareness of interdependence. Both interpret the same text, but do so according to their different situations and functions. Without the director, the designer and the actor, a play's existence is only partial. They revitalise the text with action, enabling the drama to live fully at each performance. The academic critic investigates the script to elucidate its textual problems, understand its conventions and discover how it operates. He may also propose his view of the work, expounding what he considers to be its significance.

Dramatic texts belong therefore to theatre and to literature. The aim of the 'Text and Performance' series is to achieve a fuller recognition of how both enhance our enjoyment of the play. Each volume follows the same basic pattern. Part One provides a critical introduction to the play under discussion, using the techniques and criteria of the literary critic in examining the manner in which the work operates through language, imagery and action. Part Two takes the enquiry further into the play's theatricality by focusing on selected productions of recent times so as to illustrate points of contrast and comparison in the interpretation of different directors and actors, and to demonstrate how the drama has worked on the modern stage. In this way the series seeks to provide a lively and informative introduction to major plays in their text and performance.

MICHAEL SCOTT

PLOT SYNOPSIS AND SOURCE

Othello, a black Moorish general employed by the Venetian Senate to lead its
army against the Turks, has secretly married the much younger Desdemona,
daughter of Brabantio, a respected Senator. As the play opens, his ensign
Iago capitalises on this news to get his revenge on the Moor for having, as he
claims, passed over him to promote as lieutenant a young Florentine, Michael
Cassio. Iago's first effort backfires, however, when the general and his wife
impress the Senators with their deep love for one another. Othello has orders
to avert a Turkish invasion of Cyprus, but before he departs he wins
permission to have Desdemona join him there. He entrusts her to Iago and his
wife Emilia for the voyage. A storm routs the Turks at sea, and Othello and
Desdemona are blissfully reunited in Cyprus. Here, on this outpost far from
civilisation, chance favours Iago, who soon succeeds in getting Cassio drunk
and riotous while on duty, so that Othello is forced to cashier him. Cassio's
suit to Desdemona to have her plead with Othello for his reinstatement
furnishes Iago with the pretext he is seeking to convince the Moor of his wife's
infidelity and of her 'natural' attraction to the handsome and much younger
Florentine. By planting in Cassio's quarters a lost handkerchief that Othello
had given Desdemona as a love-token, Iago ultimately is able to supply the
'ocular proof' demanded of him. Aware of his age and of his being an alien
from Venetian customs by race and culture, Othello, who 'thinks men honest
that but seem so', falls into Iago's 'net'. His ennobling love turns to a savage
passion that ends in an attempt on Cassio's life and in the murder of
Desdemona. Emilia, who originally had found the lost handkerchief, giving it
to her husband to satisfy a 'fantasy' of his, brings to light Iago's villainy.
Othello, realising the horrible injustice he has committed, now does justice
upon himself by taking his own life.

SOURCE

The main source of Othello is a lurid prose narrative by Giambattista Giraldi
Cinthio (1504–73) of Ferrara, included in his *Gli Hecatommithi* – The Hundred
Tales – published in 1565, and modelled on Boccaccio's *Decameron*. Some of
these were translated by William Painter in *Palace of Pleasure* (1566 and 1567)
though the Othello story does not appear there. A French version of it by
Gabriel Chappuys (1584) may have been used by Shakespeare. Cinthio's
Story 7 in Decade 3 of his collection is deepened, complicated and completely
transformed by Shakespeare. The outlines of the Italian story are given in
section 1 of Part One, below.

PART ONE: TEXT

1   INTRODUCTION

Characterisation and the Problem of Meaning

> But now I find I had suborned the witness
> And he's indicted falsely.   [III iv 149–50]

Othello – authentic tragic hero, or merely a tragic fool? This question dominates criticism and indicates why actors see the role as the most difficult in the Shakespearean canon to interpret and to perform. Macaulay, writing for the *Edinburgh Review* in 1827, points out how two different audiences, whether readers or spectators, might respond to Othello. The first admires 'his intrepid and ardent spirit': 'The unsuspecting confidence with which he listens to his adviser, the agony with which he shrinks from the thought of shame, the tempest of passion with which he commits his crimes, and the haughty fearlessness with which he avows them, gives an extraordinary interest to his character.' The second, however, is 'inspired with nothing but detestation and contempt' for him: 'The folly with which he trusts to the friendly professions of a man whose promotion he had obstructed, – the credulity with which he takes unsupported assertions and trivial circumstances for unanswerable proofs, – the violence with which he silences the exculpation till the exculpation can only aggravate his misery, would have excited the abhorrence and disgust of the spectators.'

The character of Othello *is* a paradox, as he himself comes to recognise at the end of the play:

> An honourable murderer, if you will:
> For naught did I in hate, but all in honour. [v ii 291–2]

This paradox divides critical opinion and even calls into question the play as a tragedy. Criticism rests uncomfortably with paradoxes and aspires to certainty. The so-called 'romantic' critics, notably A. C. Bradley (*Shakespearean Tragedy*, 1904) and Helen Gardner ('The Noble Moor', British Academy Lecture, 1956), stress the 'honourable' half of the paradox. The 'realistic' or 'anti-heroic' critics, whose major spokesman is F. R. Leavis ('Diabolic Intellect and the Noble Hero', *Scrutiny*, 6, 1937; reprinted in *The Common Pursuit*, 1952, pp. 136–59), stress 'murderer', the second and more unsavoury half. To the former Othello is the most heroic, and romantic, of Shakespeare's major tragic figures – a view regarded as mere 'sentimentality' by the latter, who consider Othello an anti-hero suffering from delusions of grandeur and excessively given to self-dramatisation. In his final speech, Othello requests the Venetian emissaries, and by implication us, to:

> Speak of me as I am: nothing extenuate,
> Nor set down aught in malice. Then must you speak
> Of one that loved not wisely, but too well;
> Of one, not easily jealous but, being wrought,
> Perplexed in the extreme; . . .   [v ii 338–42]

The romantic critics accept Othello at his word here and throughout the play; the anti-heroic critics believe with Iago that Othello's great speeches are, like this one, 'bragging and . . . fantastical lies' [II i 217].

The major critical problem of the play is, not choosing sides of a paradox, but finding a centre to Othello's character that articulates convincingly his emotional development, from the 'noble', 'valiant', 'all-in-all sufficient', and 'honourable' figure 'Whom passion could not shake' –

> . . .   Whose solid virtue
> The shot of accident nor dart of chance
> Could neither graze nor pierce . . .   [IV i 266–70]

– to the raging, insanely jealous 'murderer' of his innocent wife at the end. For the play to make sense as tragedy, Othello's death must be of a piece with his life; his plight must evoke a sympathetic response. In 'Tragedy wrought to the uttermost', Yeats writes in 'Lapis Lazuli', there is 'Gaiety transfiguring all that dread', implying that the death of the tragic hero is an occasion for 'gaiety' because it is the necessary completion of his image; it clarifies, without equivocation, the meaning of his life. 'Hamlet and Lear are gay', says the poet, but is Othello? Is his suicide a triumph of the human spirit? Or, as the anti-heroic critics claim, a desperate act, the easy way out of an intolerable situation? Even those who view it as the means of restoring a once-noble figure to his earlier and essential self, however, must explain what that essential self is.

The question has always been difficult to answer because, of Shakespeare's four great tragic heroes, Othello remains the least accessible to explanation and understanding. From the moment that we encounter Hamlet or Lear or Macbeth – on the stage or on the printed page – we enter into their tragic universes. They understand very rapidly their involvement in tragedy, and so do we; they dominate the action, and their moments of crises are adequately prepared for from the beginning. Othello, on the other hand, stands aloof from tragedy for a full half of his play; for the first two and a half acts there is nothing tragic about him. He is completely in tune with the universe, a success in love and in war, a hero out of epic and romance. More interest centres in this first half on Iago, 'the villain', as the First Folio text describes him, who has a much larger speaking role and some of the best lines, provides the play's only humour, and dominates the action. Iago constantly shifts attention away from Othello, to the point that many critics and playgoers believe that his name should title the play. Furthermore, being the only one to address us directly in soliloquies and asides, he takes us into his consciousness and thereby makes himself, if not more humanly appealing, more humanly interesting than Othello. Iago directs our responses: when he succeeds, we believe that Othello is bragging and lying. Of Iago's hatred for him Othello is totally innocent; and why should he not be? Everyone takes Iago for 'honest', and Othello has no reason to think otherwise – he even entrusts his wife to his care during the voyage to Cyprus.

As late as the start of the third act, Othello is *still* blissfully happy:

> Excellent wretch! Perdition catch my soul
> But I do love thee! And when I love thee not,
> Chaos is come again.   [III iii 90–2]

And then at some point – who can say for sure? – in the middle
of the long third scene of the act, the temptation scene, his
happiness is shattered. He listens to Iago, 'Chaos is come
again' and 'Othello's occupation's gone'. For the rest of the
play he is off on a rampage that will lead to murder and suicide.
With this scene we arrive at the crux of critical debate. At what
point does Othello change, and has the transformation been
adequately prepared so that it is plausible and convincing? To
account for the change by saying, as many have, that the play
is 'about jealousy', which needs no explanation because, as
Emilia says to Desdemona, 'They are not ever jealous for the
cause, / But jealous for they're jealous' [III iv 156–7], turns the
play into a case-history of a deranged individual rather than a
tragedy of the human situation realised through an individual
instance.

To put it in the baldest terms, unless Othello's inner agony
gets to us, unless we agree with Cassio that he is indeed 'great of
heart', we have to wonder, as a reviewer once did of a dull
performance, 'What is all the fuss about?' So much depends on
whether we see Othello as 'easily jealous' or as putting up a
struggle both against Iago and, more importantly, his own
convictions. Before he takes his life, Othello will say that he was
'not easily jealous but, being wrought, / Perplexed in the
extreme'. Unfortunately, the text can be made to yield
justification for taking Othello at his word or not. Although
many have tried, no one can say with certainty exactly where or
when in the temptation scene Othello changes. 'Each actor of
Othello', writes John Russell Brown, 'must choose the point at
which the mine is sprung within him, when he first feels and
acknowledges jealousy' (*Shakespeare's 'Othello': The Harbrace
Theatre Edition*, 1973, p. 50). For example, immediately after
Iago describes 'the green-eyed monster' of jealousy, Othello
responds, 'O misery!' [III iii 169]. The phrase is ambiguous, as
Brown points out: Othello *could* be crying out in anguish 'at his
own predicament', but he *could* just as well be reacting,
speculatively, to an idea that he had thought about before.
Similarly, a few lines later, the same ambiguity pervades
Othello's response, 'Dost thou say so?', to Iago's description of
Venetian wives who 'let God see the pranks / They dare not

show their husbands'. Both responses have their ardent
followers.

The Source and its Deployment by Shakespeare

Had Shakespeare followed more closely his main source – a
squalid tale of intrigue that Giraldi Cinthio had published in
Venice in 1565 – none of these questions of interpretation
would have arisen. Cinthio's characters are uncomplicated,
their motives are clear, and the story itself has an obvious moral
conclusion. 'Thus', says the narrator, 'did God avenge the
innocence of Disdemona [as Cinthio calls her]. . . . No less was
the Moor blamed, who had believed too foolishly. But all
praised God because the criminals had had suitable
punishment' (Geoffrey Bullough's translation, *Narrative and
Dramatic Sources of Shakespeare*, vol. 7, 1973, p. 252). Cinthio's
characters all have generic names – the Moor, the Ensign, the
Corporal, the Ensign's wife – except Disdemona, who seems to
have been given a name only so that the narrator could draw
another moral: that, since 'Disdemona' means 'unfortunate',
parents should be careful in the naming of their children. The
Moor and Disdemona marry against the wishes of her relatives,
who seem to give in and accept the marriage once it has taken
place. The couple live happily in Venice for some time before
the Moor is sent to Cyprus to command the Venetian forces
there; his appointment is a tribute to him, not a military
necessity, and is accepted as an 'honour'. The couple sail
together on 'a sea of the utmost tranquillity'. At Cyprus, the
Moor's Ensign falls 'ardently in love with Disdemona'; and,
when she fails to requite his passion, his love turns to hate, and
he plots revenge against her.

   An unexpected opportunity comes sometime later when the
Moor is forced to cashier the Corporal for wounding a soldier
on guard-duty and Disdemona pleads, without being asked, for
his reinstatement. Her concern is really for her husband who,
she feels, has lost a good friend. The Ensign tells the Moor that
the Corporal and Disdemona are lovers and that she 'has come
to dislike your blackness'. To give the Moor the proof that he

asks for, the Ensign steals a handkerchief from Disdemona and plants it in the Corporal's bed. The Corporal recognises Disdemona's handkerchief and tries to return it to her; he knocks on 'the back door' of her house, but flees when he hears the Moor's voice, thereby arousing more suspicion. Later, the Ensign takes the Moor to the Corporal's house, where, peering through a window, he sees a woman of the household copying out the pattern of the handkerchief. Convinced now of his wife's infidelity, an affront to his honour, the Moor bribes the reluctant Ensign with 'a large sum of money' to kill the Corporal, and together they execute a plan to kill Disdemona and make it look like an accident. The Ensign beats her 'with a stocking filled with sand until she dies' and with the Moor pulls down the ceiling upon her. After her death, the Moor blames his unhappiness on his Ensign, and bitter hatred develops between them. The Moor is later accused of murder and recalled to Venice to stand trial, the Ensign furnishing evidence against him, but he does not confess and is exiled. Eventually, Disdemona's relatives kill the Moor 'as he richly deserved', and the Ensign later dies a miserable death after he has been tortured for his involvement in a totally different plot. Thus the tale of the 'foolish' Moor, the 'wicked' Ensign, the 'innocent' but 'unfortunate' Disdemona, and God's vengeance upon the 'criminals'.

But what obvious moral can be drawn from *Othello*? At every turn Shakespeare complicates and mystifies where Cinthio leaves nothing to the imagination. The relatives of Cinthio's 'virtuous Lady', as we shall call her, 'did all they could to make her take another husband', but before the couple's 'mutual love' they seem to have given in, whereas Shakespeare right from the start casts suspicion on a marriage that secretly takes place in the night, without parental blessing, and that evokes violence when it is discovered. In fact, the earliest and to this day most hostile critic of the play, Thomas Rymer, judged that the playwright altered 'the Original in several particulars, but always, unfortunately, for the worse' ('A Short View of Tragedy', 1693, in *The Critical Works of Thomas Rymer*, ed. C. A. Zimansky, 1956, p. 131). Rymer is looking in the play for a nice simple moral as in Cinthio, whose 'flat' characters make easy judgements possible. But Shakespeare's complex and multi-sided characterisation makes all evidence on which to base judgements fragmentary and circumstantial; not just Othello, but all the characters in the play are paradoxes. It is small wonder that Othello begins to question whether his wife 'be honest' or not, whether Iago is 'just' or not.

For instance, although her fidelity, her innocence, is never in question to us, an open and frank sexuality emanates from Desdemona that at least renders plausible Iago's hold on Othello and holds out hope for Roderigo. Cinthio felt it necessary to tell his readers that the 'virtuous Lady of wondrous beauty' was 'impelled not by female appetite but by the Moor's good qualities' to fall in love with him. But, as Alfred Harbage points out, 'Shakespeare makes no such apology' (*As They Liked It*, 1947, p. 65). Othello assures the Venetian Senators that, in taking Desdemona with him to Cyprus, he does so not to 'please the palate of my appetite' but only 'to be free and bounteous to her mind' [I iii 257 ff.]. He is telling them only a half-truth, for as soon as he and Desdemona are reunited at Cyprus he cannot wait to enjoy the 'fruits' and 'profit' between them. Throughout the play his 'sense aches' at her 'sweetness' – nowhere more hauntingly so than at the beginning of the final scene where her physical beauty distracts him from the ritual 'sacrifice' that he has come to perform. Desdemona, however, is more frank with the Senators. She does not want to remain behind in Venice 'A moth of peace', for should Othello go to Cyprus without her 'The rites for which I love him are bereft me, / And I a heavy interim shall support / By his dear absence' [I iii 252–6].

Harbage informs us that 'in the popular mind of Shakespeare's time' the 'only' explanation for Desdemona's attraction to Othello, black-skinned and much older, had to be 'the waywardness of lust'. And it is exactly by this argument – much more so than by the later 'ocular proof' of the handkerchief – that Iago mainly convinces Othello of her lust; he makes him see the marriage as 'unnatural'. Othello himself has opened the way for Iago by noting 'how nature erring from itself –', whereupon Iago interrupts to develop the argument:

> Ay, there's the point: as to be bold with you,
> Nor to affect many proposèd matches
> Of her own clime, complexion, and degree,

> Whereto we see in all things nature tends,
> Foh! One may smell in such a will most rank,
> Foul disproportion, thoughts unnatural.   [III iii 225–31]

Cinthio's Lady herself comes to the conclusion, as Desdemona never does, that her marriage may have been a mistake: 'I fear greatly that I shall be a warning to young girls not to marry against their parents' wishes; and Italian ladies will learn by my example not to tie themselves to a man whom Nature, Heaven, and manner of life separate from us.' But, although the Ensign tells the Moor that his wife has come 'to dislike your blackness', the only actual reference to colour in the work, Cinthio never portrays the Moor as physically repulsive or indicates any disparity in his and the Lady's ages. Not only is Othello 'declined / Into the vale of years', but the total physical portrait of him, as the husband of Desdemona, is meant to arouse distaste – 'an old black ram', 'the thick-lips', 'the sooty bosom', 'what she feared to look on'. These words come from Iago and Roderigo and Brabantio, who have their own fixations about Othello, but they are not for that reason to be discounted. We are not meant to picture a couple handsomely matched in years and looks, the typical lovers of romantic comedy. Cinthio's lovers come closer to the stereotype.

The most astonishing sea-change from narrative to drama is that of the Ensign, motivated solely by lust for the Lady and revenge against her when his passion is unrequited, to Iago, motivated – by what? Lack of promotion? Racial prejudice? Hatred of the foreigner (Florentines, like Cassio, as well as Moors)? Class hatred? Sexual jealousy or even sexual inadequacy? The 'daily beauty' of those who make him 'ugly'? Iago himself makes most of these motives explicit, and others can be inferred from his dialogue. All plausible motives, but they do not add up to the havoc that he causes. He tosses out his motives so haphazardly and so unexpectedly at various moments in the play – the 'daily beauty' excuse appears in the next to the last scene – that they have the effect of cancelling each other out. To many Iago actually appears 'motiveless'. The first reason that he gives for hating Othello and Cassio, his lack of promotion, makes him appear credible where credibility is most needed – at the start of the play. But this motive is soon forgotten as others take its place. Explanations of Iago seem endless, but Iago is finally unexplainable with any certainty. His final words are:

> Demand me nothing; what you know, you know:
> From this time forth I never will speak word. [v ii 300–1]

And he does not. We know only what we have seen and heard, but our interpretations must always remain problematic. Iago's actions, not his motives, explain him. No recourse to his representing Evil Personified, a Vice figure, or the Devil himself in human clothing is necessary. Iago's humanity is frightening in itself, and his Jekyll outside and Hyde inside are reasons enough that Othello and the others do not see through him.

Cinthio's Corporal is just a pawn in the Ensign's scheme to take revenge upon the Lady, but transformed into Cassio he is in some ways a complex and baffling figure. Iago envies him his 'daily beauty' [v i 19], but if that means anything more than personal good looks – in contrast to Othello's looks, and reason enough for Othello to feel jealous of him – the play nowhere makes clear. Shakespeare endows Cassio with many obvious attractive qualities, such as his noble appreciation of Desdemona's womanhood, his unwavering loyalty to his 'dear general', his acceptance of personal responsibility for his wrongdoing while on military duty (he never claims that he was cashiered unjustly), and his subsequent sorrow and repentance. But a certain shabbiness also characterises him, as in his condescension to Iago ('The Lieutenant is to be saved before the Ancient' [ii iii 104–5]), in his persistent efforts to involve Desdemona on his behalf, and in his belittling of Bianca, who is described in the First Folio text as a 'Curtezan' but whose devotion to him seems clearly not mercenary. Iago describes Cassio as an inexperienced, 'bookish' sort of soldier, 'a great arithmetician' [i i 19], who, if life were fairer, would not have been promoted above him to the lieutenancy; but Desdemona informs us [iii iv 93] that he 'Shared dangers' with Othello. The play never spells out whether Othello appointed him his lieutenant for his military skills or out of friendship, but the Venetian Senators deem him a suitable replacement for Othello as governor of Cyprus even before they hear of the tragic events on that island. Early in the play, in conversing with Iago, he seems not to know that his general is married or to whom [1 ii 52], but later Desdemona again informs us how he 'came a-wooing' with Othello. Not only that, he often took Othello's part when, as she admits, she spoke 'dispraisingly' of him [III iii 71–4].

All kinds of suggestions have been put forth to explain the discrepancies in Cassio's characterisation, as they have for every character in the play. Is Cassio pretending ignorance about the marriage because he does not wish to discuss it with Iago, an inferior in rank and possibly in class? Is the text itself flawed? Has Shakespeare simply forgotten? The point of all these and countless other questions about *Othello* is that the text constantly seems to be inviting us to go outside of it for explanations, none of which is ever, in the final analysis, truly satisfactory.

The questions keep multiplying, and along with them the suggested answers. Some of the changes from Cinthio to Shakespeare may be the normal result of compressing a narrative that occurs over a lengthy period of time to drama – as the shortened time scheme; the compression of events, as Othello's death by his own hand in Cyprus rather than the need for a trial scene in Venice and his subsequent killing by his wife's family; the elimination of unnecessary characters, as the Ensign's three-year-old daughter whom the Lady is holding while the Ensign steals her handkerchief; the condensation of several characters into one, as the Lady's relatives into Desdemona's father, the Corporal's mistress and the woman of his household who copies out the design on the handkerchief into Bianca.

Some of the problems involving interpretation of individual lines or passages may be due to the way that the printed text has come down to us. Something like over a thousand major variants exist between the First Quarto of 1622 and the First Folio text of 1623. One theory has it that these major differences reflect Shakespeare's own revisions and tampering with the text over the years, but we can never know. The changes that the playwright made in his source material and the problems of interpretation that the play poses are too many and too pervasive to be explained solely by dramatic necessity or by faulty textual transmission or by the playwright's carelessness.

Comparing Cinthio's tale with Shakespeare's play is no mere academic exercise, for the comparison makes abundantly clear that the playwright consistently, at every opportunity, deepened and complicated his source as part of a conscious design to mystify. The world of *Othello* is one of uncertainty and indeterminacy, where the 'shot of accident' and the 'dart of chance' hold sway. The Ensign steals the handkerchief as part of a carefully laid plan; luck brings it to Iago [III iii]. The Ensign takes the Moor to where he can see the handkerchief; Bianca comes walking in with it at an opportune moment for Iago [III iv]. What Rymer did not understand is that, by altering 'the Original', Shakespeare was not just changing narrative to drama but actually making dramatic form itself the means of enhancing sympathy for Othello: sympathy that becomes more meaningful than any statement of what the play is 'about' and raises Othello to a figure of tragic significance. Drama creates the illusion of life as it is actually lived. It resists doctrinaire or abstract interpretations that never match the flux of reality and the varying, even contradictory, impressions that people make upon others in their ordinary lives. How much, after all, is it given to any of us to know our own motives or those of others?

Shakespeare's method of characterisation in *Othello* is such that we can never fully understand anyone in the play. As in life itself, we have to piece together bits of information, circumstantial evidence, hoping to understand – Iago's motive one moment, his motive at another; what Cassio says in one place, how he contradicts himself in another; why Emilia knows where the handkerchief is and says nothing; why Desdemona can be both 'A maiden never bold' and one who trumpets to the world her 'downright violence and storm of fortunes'; and, of course, why Othello may be justified in calling himself 'An honourable murderer'. Iago thinks that he knows everything, that he is masterminding a plot; but the plot masterminds him in the end. The handkerchief is his undoing. We see, of course, much more than Othello sees; but, knowing that we cannot know everything, we are in a better position to sympathise with Othello, who, like us, encounters a world beyond understanding. Because every character reveals so many sides, often hidden from others in the play, that reflect the rich and varied particularities of life itself, Othello's confusion about Desdemona and his misplaced trust in Iago become more comprehensible. In sympathy begins understanding.

2   STRUCTURE AS MEANING

> . . . the net / That shall enmesh them all   [II iii 351–2]

The dramatic illusion of life that Shakespeare renders so vividly in *Othello* is, of course, only an illusion. Because of its life-likeness, the play constantly invites interpretation outside and beyond the dramatic action. Drama, however, counters the seeming formlessness or 'chaos' of life with design. Action tests character, and character analyses divorced from the design of the play are misleading, especially when individual lines or scenes are cited or examined in isolation from the whole. To take just one example: how do we explain Othello's cashiering of Cassio at the end of the second act – as a rash act by an 'incredulous fool'? or as an act of military responsibility on an island still threatened by war and mutiny? This scene, like so many others, has to be seen in context of the whole.

The major problem of interpretation is accounting for the change in Othello that occurs in the temptation scene [III iii]. The play's emotional balance leads up to and descends from this pivotal scene. For the change to be convincing, the structure of the play must *sweep* us into unhesitating belief so that we never lose our sympathetic understanding of Othello or fail to see him, rather than Iago, as the centre of the action. The first thing that we must recognise is that the play has no natural five-act structure. What makes it possible for us, readers or spectators, to be swept along emotionally is the play's tightly interlocking sequence of scenes that allows for no natural break or interval. The structure itself is a 'net' that enmeshes us.

The practice of dividing *Othello* into five acts began with the First Folio of 1623; but the First Quarto, published the year before, is, in its haphazard attempt to divide it only into Act II,

scene i, Act IV, and Act V, probably closer to the playwright's
intention not to have any division at all. Off-hand, the Folio
division between Acts I and II does have a certain *narrative* logic:
the action at civilised Venice is now over, and a new phase is
about to begin on Venus's 'warlike isle' of Cyprus. The first act
(to use such designations for ease of reference only) ends with
Iago, alone, just beginning to give shape to his as-yet-uncertain
plans 'To get [Cassio's] place and to plume up my will / In
double knavery'. His last words are: 'I have't. It is engendered.
Hell and night / Must bring this monstrous birth to light.'
What immediately follows is the crashing storm that opens the
second act, as if Iago's incantation were directly responsible for
it:

> Methinks the wind does speak aloud at land;
> A full blast ne'er shook our battlements.
> . . .
> The wind-shaked surge, with high and monstrous mane,
> Seems to cast water on the burning Bear
> And quench the guards of th'ever-fixèd Pole.
> I never did like molestation view
> On the enchafèd flood.   [II i 5–17]

Any interval between Acts I and II destroys the effect of Iago's
'monstrous birth'. Like so much else in the play, the storm takes
on double meanings: it routs the Turkish fleet and brings the
Venetians and their general to victory and safety; but, coming
as it does directly on the words of Iago, it foreshadows the storm
to come in the play's interior or emotional drama. It had been
anticipated in Desdemona's avowal, also in the final scene of
the first act (line 246), that her marriage to Othello trumpets to
the world her 'downright violence and storm of fortunes'.
Cinthio's Moor and his Lady sail together to Cyprus on 'a sea of
the utmost tranquillity'; Othello and Desdemona separately
come through the natural storm with ease, but Iago's 'monstrous' storm is another matter, one that they will not be able to
negotiate.

   At the beginning of Act II, Iago's knavish plans are 'but yet
confused' [II i 302]. By the end of that act, having rather easily
effected Cassio's dismissal, Iago now sees clearly the way
before him and recognises that he must 'Dull not device by

coldness and delay' [II iii 377] – the leisurely time of Cinthio's narrative would work against him. The beginning of Act III stresses the continuity from the previous act and how quickly, indeed, Iago has set about his diabolic work. Day had broken before Iago and Cassio parted at the end of the preceding act, and Act III opens with the latter's having lost no time in following Iago's advice of Act II to solicit Emilia's, and through her Desdemona's, aid in regaining his position. Iago, apparently not having been to bed either, is on hand to egg Cassio on:

IAGO   You have not been abed then?
CASS.   Why, no: the day had broke before we parted.
        I have made bold, Iago,
        To send in to your wife. My suit to her
        Is that she will to virtuous Desdemona
        Procure me some access.   [III i 30–5]

At the end of Act III, Cassio tells Bianca, his mistress, to leave him, for he does not want Othello to see him 'womaned', not realising, of course, that Othello now thinks that he already has been 'womaned' with Desdemona. In the opening scene of Act IV, Cassio unknowingly *is* 'womaned' with Bianca, bearing Desdemona's handkerchief, in Othello's sight. The break between Acts IV and V is also unnatural. The so-called willow or bedchamber scene between Desdemona and Emilia [IV iii] is, as Carol Thomas Neely points out, the only scene of genuine friendship in the entire play and is sadly and ironically 'sandwiched between two exchanges of Iago and Roderigo' [IV ii & v i] ('Women and Men in *Othello* . . .', *Shakespeare Studies 10*, 1977, pp. 144–5). The scene, even as it emphasises Desdemona's unswerving devotion to Othello ('my love doth so approve him', line 18), also falls between the brothel scene [IV ii] in which Othello accuses Desdemona of being a whore and Emilia her bawd, and the scene in which he is on his way to kill her ('Strumpet, I come!' [v i 34]). In the second and final scene of Act V, Othello murders Desdemona on the bed to which she was preparing to retire in the final scene of the fourth act. The first scene of Act V, with its brutal murder of Roderigo and near assassination of Cassio, on which Othello for a few moments looks with gusto (lines 31–6), also lends weight to Desdemona's premonitions of death at the end of Act IV and furnishes an ironic commentary on the last scene which starts out with the dignity of a ritual 'sacrifice' but rapidly turns to the violence of murder.

At the very centre, literally, of these interconnecting scenes that constitute the structure of the play, Othello moves from a non-tragic to a tragic world. Eight scenes, as the play now is divided, precede the great temptation scene of the third act, and six follow; but, of the first eight, two hardly qualify as scenes at all – the eleven-line 'proclamation scene' [II ii], which in the First Folio is combined with the next scene, and the six-line 'fortifications scene' [III ii]. The temptation episode itself [sc. iii] is a direct continuation of the first scene of Act III. There, at the end, Emilia promises to take Cassio to Desdemona, and they leave the stage. The brief fortifications scene that follows, in which Othello dismisses Iago and proceeds with 'Gentlemen' to inspect the fortifications of Cyprus, allows time for Emilia and Cassio to go their way and re-emerge, just six lines later at the beginning of the next scene, with Desdemona. The fortifications scene is striking for the glimpse – no more than that – that it affords us, for the last time in the play, of Othello fully in command of himself and secure in his 'occupation'. Sandwiched between the two scenes of Cassio's coming to plead his suit [III i & III iii], it comments favourably on Othello as a responsible leader who had been forced to cashier Cassio at the end of the previous act for neglecting his professional duties. After giving orders to Iago, Othello dismisses him; but, just twenty-eight lines later into the next scene, Othello reappears with Iago, who at once begins to rouse him to suspicion and jealousy as they witness Cassio's departure in shame from Desdemona. By the end of this long and taut scene, which the hostile Thomas Rymer ruefully admitted 'raises *Othello* above all other Tragedies on our Theatres', the general and his ensign kneel together in a vow that mocks the marriage ceremony:

OTH.   . . .   Now art thou my Lieutenant.
IAGO   I am your own for ever.   [III iii 475–6]

As we noted earlier, each interpreter of the scene has to decide at exactly which point Othello feels the onrush of jealousy and anger, but the very length of the scene suggests that Othello is no easy victim. Iago, blessed by fortune at the beginning of the scene with Cassio's sudden 'guilty-like' departure, has to work ever more feverishly, as Othello becomes more desperate and even violent, the substitute his appearance of 'honesty' for the 'ocular proof' that is demanded of him and that he knows cannot exist. In fact, speaking of Desdemona and Cassio, he tells Othello as much:

> It were a tedious difficulty, I think,
> To bring them to that prospect. Damn them then
> If ever mortal eyes do see them bolster
> More than their own! What then? How then?
> What shall I say? Where's satisfaction?
> It is impossible you should see this, . . .   [III iii 394–9]

Only the methods of 'imputation and strong circumstance' are left to Iago. Despite his proud boast that 'on the proof, there is no more but this: / Away at once with love or jealousy!' [189–90], Othello never stops struggling against the love that he so deeply feels and cannot relinquish. If it were otherwise, he would be able to say to Desdemona something similar to what he had said earlier to Cassio: 'Cassio, I love thee, / But nevermore be officer of mine' [II iii 242–3]. Othello, however, is not able to cashier his 'fair warrior', his 'captain's captain', so easily. More than three-quarters through the scene, he registers confusion in two of the play's most poignant lines:

> I think my wife be honest, and think she is not;
> I think that thou art just, and think thou art not.
>   [III iii 381–2]

To which Iago responds a few lines later, 'I see, sir, you are eaten up with passion' – an implicit stage direction indicating how Othello 'reads' his lines: words and gestures are here meant to support his inner agony. By the end of the scene, Iago's triumph may seem total, but he, too, is unwittingly weaving himself into, as he says, 'the net / That shall enmesh them all'. Cinthio's Ensign deliberately had devised a plan to steal the handkerchief from the Lady, but the handkerchief that comes to Iago in the middle of the scene by a stroke of fortune will in the final scene entrap him too. The world of 'accident' and 'chance' operates on him as much as on the 'credulous fools' and 'asses' he takes everyone else to be.

To have an interval or break between this scene and the next [III iv] is to obscure a splendid irony. The final words of the temptation scene are Iago's 'I am your own for ever' – and, immediately, in the next scene, enters Desdemona, who has made, as Othello has, the same vow in marriage and who, as in her defence of Cassio, will 'perform it / To the last article'. Furthermore, so tight is the net that Shakespeare himself is weaving in his dramatic design that, as one scene leads into the next, any interval threatens to lessen the on-going tension. The fourth scene of Act III, in which Othello demands the handkerchief from Desdemona in his astonishing, and to her incomprehensible, 'magic in the web' speech [55–75], reveals at once how swiftly Iago's 'medicine' has taken effect. From now until the end of the play, Othello's 'fury', as Desdemona calls it, never abates. At the beginning of the play's final scene, even the outward calm with which he approaches the bridal bed, now a sacrificial bed to him, is deceptive. Desdemona's warm defence of her innocence and her alarms over Cassio's supposed death only reawaken the demon in him, turning what he 'thought a sacrifice' into murder.

If Iago, meanwhile, is being driven to taking more and more chances as the net tightens, Shakespeare seems to be taking even greater risks in this second half of the play by presenting a 'hero' who comes dangerously close to resembling the jealous cuckold of traditional comedy or farce, the older husband married to the much younger wife. After the temptation scene, maintaining the sympathetic interest that Othello should evoke is a major feat. For many critics a tension between tragedy and comedy in the play creates a strange feeling of dislocation.

As early as 1693, Thomas Rymer judged *Othello* to be, in fact, not a tragedy at all but 'a Bloody Farce, without salt or savour'. Too much, he thought, hinged, as in farce, on 'so remote a trifle' as a handkerchief: 'Had it been *Desdemona*'s Garter, the Sagacious Moor might have smelt a Rat.' Othello's 'Love' and 'Jealousie' Rymer considered subjects fit only for comedy, and Othello himself he thought just a 'jealous Booby' (pp. 154, 160, 164). Rymer's 'Bloody Farce' finds its modern counterparts in descriptions like 'cankered comedy' or 'a very comic tragedy, if a tragedy at all'. Even sympathetic critics, like Helen Gardner, have observed the play's 'affinity with comedy'. Unlike the other major Shakespearean tragedies, *Othello* has more in common with the world of Shakespeare's comedies and sonnets in its emphasis on the power and vicissitudes of love, its domestic rather than dynastic ambience, the large element of intrigue, the many points of view, the fun with word-playing, and the concern with masks and self-identity. Moreover, from the end of the temptation scene until the final scene, Othello, in his lunatic refusal to listen to any arguments from Desdemona – or Emilia or Cassio – that might release him from his jealous fixation, seems to bear some resemblance to the 'humours' husbands of Jonson and Molière.

The carry-over of comic structure and the archetypal characters of comedy – the old husband and his young wife and her young lover, the threatening father, the mischievous servant – into *The Tragedy of Othello, the Moor of Venice* (to cite the play's full title) is, however, not all that surprising. Latent in all of Shakespeare's comedies, amid the high jinks and genuine fun of the battle of the sexes, is the fearful sense of love's vulnerability. Not just those of a different race or culture, like a Moor of Venice (a contradiction in terms), but *all* lovers are ultimately outsiders – the main implication of Othello's blackness amid all whites since one's identity in love, one's own personal esteem, depends so much on another. The ultimate hurt to which love exposes us is cuckoldry. The bawdy jokes and puns scattered throughout the romantic comedies generally reflect a healthy attitude toward sex – Desdemona's attitude without the bawdy. But in the later so-called 'problem plays', particularly in *Troilus and Cressida*, the jokes become uglier and, as in *Othello*, reflect a more corrosive vision. Nevertheless, a good marriage is a personal triumph for the lovers; it preserves or restores the social order and in the comedies is the 'journey's end' [cf. *Oth.*, v ii 265]. In *Othello* it is just the beginning of the journey, and from the start of the play the resonating context of the earlier romantic comedies establishes and clarifies the depth and triumph of Othello's love. Because that love does not have to be proved, most of the early scenes leisurely display Othello victorious in love as in war. With the temptation scene, in the middle of the play, the pace speeds up, inexorably, towards the catastrophe and resolution. The two halves of the play move at much different paces.

Othello makes his entrance into the play as a figure out of the romance or even epic tradition in literature, not as the *commedia dell'arte* 'pantaloon' that he verges on becoming in the second half. Iago's sordid, racist description of him in the first scene establishes the traditional Elizabethan stage Moor, like Shakespeare's own Aaron in *Titus Andronicus*, his blackness associated with the devil and with lasciviousness. But Othello's appearance in the second scene belies any stereotyped figure. His first words – ''Tis better as it is' [I ii 6], in answer to Iago's provocative remarks about Brabantio – give the lie by their simplicity and calm dignity to Iago's portrait and contrast sharply with Iago's verbosity: the verbosity of an accomplished hypocrite! In the opening scene, Iago provokes chaos, noise, confusion; in the second, Othello establishes order merely by being himself. 'Keep up your bright swords, for the dew will rust them' is all he needs to say to stop the fighting at once. In the third scene of the first act, Othello's self-confidence, not 'self-glorification', comes from the assurance that Desdemona's love gives him: 'Send for the lady to the Sagittary, / And let her speak of me before her father' [I iii 115–16]. He is willing to accept death if the Senate finds him 'foul in her report', and it is only after she addresses that body that he refers to her for the first time simply as 'my wife'. In spite of what Iago and Brabantio and Roderigo say, Othello stands to gain no material advantage – the 'fortune' that Roderigo refers to in the act's first scene [67] – from this marriage. Their secret marriage alone ensures that.

Reunited on Cyprus at the beginning of Act II, after a separation immediately following their marriage, the two lovers enjoy their happiest moment in the play. Cinthio's lovers sailed together on 'a sea of the utmost tranquillity', but Shakespeare separates them only to demonstrate in their reunion the intensity of their love. Free of the restraint proper to the Venetian Senate, they embrace and kiss, able to acknowledge publicly the sensual attraction that each has for the other. A short second scene, if it can be called that, follows in which the Herald reads aloud Othello's proclamation of victory over the Turks and the celebration of his nuptials. The act's final

scene – with the cashiering of Cassio – is a vivid display of the
promise Othello had given earlier to the Senators: that even
with Desdemona at his side, he would never 'scant' their
'serious and great business' [I iii 263–5]. Like Desdemona, he is
true to his word.

The cashiering of Cassio is one of the more troubling
instances in the play of how Shakespeare makes judgement
difficult, for us as well as for Othello. The scene has to be
troubling because we know what no one else in the scene,
except Iago, knows – that the riot was concocted by Iago, who,
like the Turks earlier, but more successfully, has wrought 'a
pageant / To keep us in false gaze' [see I iii 18–19]. The scene
had begun with Othello's ordering Cassio to command the
guard that night but not to 'outsport discretion' since the island
is still at war, despite the temporary lull, and mutiny is feared.
When Othello next appears, 'raised up' from his slumbers with
Desdemona, mutiny in fact is being proclaimed, the warning
bell is sounding, and Cassio has wounded the much-respected
former governor of the island, Montano. The military situation
demands swift judgement. Even without Iago's 'explanation'
(which, it should be noted, both Cassio and Montano accept),
Othello has the new governor all the 'ocular proof' that he
needs. That he only half means what he says to Cassio, 'I love
thee, / But nevermore be officer of mine', is borne out in the next
scene, the first of Act III, when Emilia reports to Cassio that
Othello had no choice but to 'refuse' him since Montano 'is of
great fame in Cyprus, / And great affinity'; the general, she goes
on to say, 'protests he loves you' and upon 'the safest occasion'
will reinstate his former lieutenant [III i 40–9]. Had Cassio been
patient, Desdemona's intercession on his behalf would have
been unnecessary. As it is, he is reluctant to pursue the course
that Iago has advised, and only persuasion makes him go on:
'There is no other way', says Iago; 'Go, and importune her' [III
iv 103–4].

Thus, although Iago's ironic perspective modifies what we
see and hear, the structure of the first half of the play slowly
builds up an impressive portrait of its hero. In the noisy,
brawling public scenes manufactured by Iago and before the
Senate, Othello shines in his 'occupation', as he calls it. The
rapid disintegration of the 'noble' and 'valiant' Moor from the

middle of the play on takes him from that public non-tragic world to the desolatingly quiet, private, and tragic world symbolised on Shakespeare's scenery-less stage by the only prop that *Othello* absolutely requires: the bed at the opening of the play's final scene. Cinthio's Moor never learns of his wife's innocence, and her family takes revenge upon him. Othello's suicide, in contrast, is in keeping with his heroic character. Having told Brabantio, 'My life upon her faith!' [i iii 291], Othello keeps his word in a public act of justice that marks the restoration of his true self. If there is 'Gaiety transfiguring all that dread', as Yeats said, it comes from Othello's recognition that his essential self resided in Desdemona and that his faith in her had always been justified.

3   LANGUAGE AS ACTION

> These sentences, to sugar or to gall
> Being strong on both sides, are equivocal. [i iii 214–15]

The key to Othello is language. In it lies the centre that articulates his emotional development from a romantic to a tragic figure. Because of the constantly shifting perspectives of the play, it is easy to interpret anything that Othello says equivocally. To do so, however, is to overlook the important consideration of structure, and Othello's place in it, and to examine language in isolation. In the final scene, Emilia shouts to Othello, 'O gull! O dolt!/ As ignorant as dirt!' [v ii 162–3], and many have praised her as the 'voice of reality'. But, when we start talking about 'reality', we ourselves confront the inadequacy of language in normal discourse. What Emilia says at this particular moment is true enough, but her words hardly begin to define the totality of Othello's character. Is what Othello says in this scene and throughout the play 'unreal'? In a famous passage in 'Shakespeare and the Stoicism of Seneca' (1927), T. S. Eliot called into question the sincerity of Othello's final speech and opened the way for the modern denigration of all his great speeches:

I have always felt that I have never read a more terrible exposure of
human weakness – of universal human weakness – than the last
great speech of Othello. . . . It it usually taken on its face value, as
expressing the greatness in defeat of a noble but erring nature. . . .
What Othello seems to me to be doing in making this speech is
cheering himself up. He is endeavouring to escape reality, he has
ceased to think about Desdemona, and is thinking about himself.
. . . Othello succeeds in turning himself into a pathetic figure, by
adopting an *aesthetic* rather than a moral attitude, dramatizing
himself against his environment. (*Selected Essays*, 3rd edn, 1951, pp.
130–1)

Many readers have extended Eliot's view to include almost
everything that Othello says.

What Eliot and his followers are doing, however, is reading a
script that Iago, not Shakespeare, has written. Iago dominates
the first half of the play, and through his soliloquies he mediates
between us and the other characters. In effect, he becomes a
playwright-within-the-play. Simply as playwrights, he and
Shakespeare share the same goal: to create the dramatic
illusion of reality from mere *words*. 'It is not words that shake
me thus!', Othello cries out near the end of a passage of utter
verbal confusion [IV i 41], just moments before he 'falls in a
trance' (the First Folio stage direction). But he is deadly wrong.
Iago now stands gloating over him: 'Work on, / My medicine' –
his 'poison' actually, which is neither more nor less than
language itself. With words only he has successfully enmeshed
Othello in his net. On emerging from his trance, Othello, at his
ensign's instigation, 'encaves' himself, presumably behind one
of the two stage pillars on the Globe stage, and proceeds
immediately to 'misread' – which at this moment also means
'mis-see' – the scenario that Iago has concocted between
himself and Cassio as they banter about the latter's 'customer'
or whore, Bianca, while Othello thinks that they are laughing
at Desdemona. Language dictates even what he sees.

Of all the characters in the play Iago is the only one who
understands the arbitrary nature of language as an endlessly
manipulable system of signs that are social and cultural in
origin. As master-manipulator of signs, Iago throws into
confusion the language of discourse, to the point where Othello
does not know what to think anymore: whether his wife is

'honest', whether Iago is 'just'. Iago's success in manoeuvring Othello and others to 'read' the world by his own signs is largely attributable to his conscious manipulation of himself as a 'sign': 'I am not what I am', he admits [I i 66], an admission that he can afford to make because 'honesty' is his strategy.

If language, however, is what enables us to create our sense of reality, Iago's total appropriation (or, more properly, disappropriation) of the language of discourse creates the very 'chaos' that Othello's love of Desdemona has overcome [see III iii 90–2]. Signs – words – only signify; they cannot be the equivalent of what or whom they are signifying. What makes communication possible is a faith in language that bridges that silent gap between the word and what it refers to. Love 'speaks' in that silence. But Iago demystifies language. He speaks in that gap by totally objectifying it. The world for him is a body to be read literally, not a mystery to be accepted and interpreted with love and humility. There are no mysteries for Iago, to whom all Moors are lascivious, all women are whores, and all men, except himself, of course, are asses. Under his spell Othello claims not words shake him but 'Noses, ears, and lips!' [IV i 42]. For Iago, black is black and white is white, and his greatest triumph is to make Othello accept his literal blackness as the reality of his being whereas previously Desdemona had awakened him to his full humanity by seeing his 'visage in his mind' [I iii 249]. Desdemona's 'love' does not depend on external signs as Iago's 'hate' does. He confesses that to deceive Othello, 'I must show out a flag and sign of love' [I i 157]. Desdemona gives the lie to Iago; to believe in his world as 'real' is to believe in a world drained of meaning, one that is 'merely a lust of the blood and a permission of the will' [I iii 331–2]. Before she leaves him at the start of the temptation scene, Desdemona says to Othello, 'Be as your fancies teach you. / Whate'er you be, I am obedient' [III iii 88–9]. Unfortunately, she leaves him to the 'fancies' that Iago now starts teaching him, and Othello's acceptance of them is acceptance of a lunatic world where even time is out of joint: hardly a couple of days on Cyprus and he believes 'That she with Cassio hath the act of shame / A thousand times committed' [v ii 210–11].

Iago as playwright uses language to imprison characters: Shakespeare, however, uses it to set them free in all their

mysterious individuality and thereby strengthens our sense of
reality. Both deal in surfaces, which is the way that we see
others in everyday life, but only Shakespeare suggests depths.
Eliot admits as much when he says that Othello 'takes in the
spectator' as well as himself; the history of criticism and of
performance reveals that most of us want to be on Othello's
side. Iago's reductive and Shakespeare's liberating views of
language clash most overtly in the 'scripts' that each writes for
Othello, whose speech before the Senate [I iii 127–69] and his
final speech [v ii 334–52], in particular, have come to stand as
test cases for any interpretation of character and meaning. Both
speeches, with their similar cadences and simplicity of
phrasing, suggest comparison; but the 'journey' between them
reveals why Othello in truth can say as he nears the end of his
life that he has nowhere to go. In the final speech he is and at the
same time he is not the Othello of the Senate speech. Neither
'romantic' nor 'realistic' adequately describes him at this point.

Before he addresses the Senators, Othello, in what might be
called a 'peroration' to his speech [I iii 76–94], promises to
deliver 'a round unvarnished tale . . . / Of my whole course of
love' and apologises beforehand for being 'Rude . . . in my
speech / And little blessed with the soft phrase of peace'. That
Othello – as an alien in Venice, indicated so strikingly by his
physical blackness, and on trial – should feel the need to ease
his way into his defence is hardly a matter of blame. But aware,
too, that the courtly language of Venice is also alien to him, he
is asking his auditors to look upon his words as signs only, to
look beyond them to find the real Othello. ('Look with thine
ears', as King Lear says in Shakespeare's next play.) That the
tale he proceeds to tell communicates itself as anything but
'rude' or 'unvarnished' is due largely to the effect that the very
telling has on him, so that as he recounts his courtship of
Desdemona he is also reliving it. The speech is dramatic, not
histrionic: the narrator becomes indistinguishable from the
narration, and for a time that gap between language and desire
is successfully bridged. 'Rude' and 'unvarnished' transform
themselves into a dignified plainness and an unadorned
simplicity that strike a note of sincerity so obviously missing
from the twisted and contradictory speeches of Iago (see the
next section). The speech reflects a harmony between language

and psyche that moves – or should move – Othello's listeners to look, indeed, beyond the *signs* of discourse and of skin colour to see the 'visage in his mind' that Desdemona saw.

As Othello tells his tale, something is happening to him; he is being caught up in his own narration, which seems to transform him in the process of being told. The speech operates on two levels as it recounts the past and re-enacts it in the present, combining past and present into a perfect moment that transcends time. Critics have maintained that the speech is not very passionate, which is true; the passion will come later. It re-enacts, however, something more profound than passion: the discovery of love. Hitherto Othello's life had been no more than a catalogue of events, one thing after another – 'disastrous chances', 'moving accidents', 'hair-breadth scapes', captivity and 'slavery', 'redemption' and 'travels' – exciting but as meaningless and empty as the 'antres vast and deserts idle' that he mentions. The speech would remain a mere catalogue, a 'chaos' of happenings, were it not received, as he says, by Desdemona's 'greedy ear'. The closure of Othello's narration by Desdemona's love turns his life into a work of art, an ordered whole with beginning, middle, and a 'journey's end' in Desdemona, who completes his narration as interpreter so that his story exists in her and, by implication, in us. Her love gives him genuine identity by liberating him from the stereotyped identifications of Iago, Brabantio and Roderigo. And, paradoxically, the bond of matrimony furnishes his life with a centre that sets him free to be his own true self. He exists in Desdemona's love, which, out of modesty and surprise at his own good fortune, he interprets as 'pity' although she makes clear not many lines later that her feelings are more engaged: 'My heart's subdued / Even to the very quality of my lord' [I iii 247–8].

Once Iago's words begin to shake him, Othello's loss of faith in himself corresponds to a loss of faith in language; he begins to demand literalism. The handkerchief that Rymer so much objected to now becomes a matter of exaggerated importance. "Tis true: there's magic in the web of it', he says to an astonished Desdemona, who does not begin to comprehend what he is talking about [III iv 55–82]. To her the lost handkerchief is a token or sign of his love. But, in equating the loss of that token with the loss of love itself, Othello is literally converting a sign into what it signifies and thereby is destroying its true significance. By the beginning of the final scene, the gap between his words and what they signify is at its most glaring. About to take Desdemona's life, he has convinced himself that his private revenge is strictly a public duty, but Desdemona's physical beauty keeps unhinging him: 'O balmy breath, that dost almost persuade / Justice to break her sword!' [v ii 16–17]. At this point he 'reads' her body but not her spirit. Desdemona's own last words, in which she takes blame for her murder, are cryptic: 'Nobody – I myself – farewell. / Commend me to my kind lord – O, farewell!' [125–6]. 'My kind lord' is the Othello whose 'visage' she saw 'in his mind'; her 'Nobody' could be only the 'false', stereotypical Moor as Othello is now. The effect of these words is to remind Othello of what he knew when he addressed the Senate: that words, or signs, mean more than they say. As he now begins to abandon Iago's literalism, remorse follows swiftly.

Later in the final scene Othello acknowledges his divided self: 'That's he that was Othello: here I am' [v ii 281]. His last speech, however, brings 'words and performances' [see IV ii 182–3] together again, culminating in the suicide that marks the return of his 'occupation'. Taking his life is not a cowardly act or escape from reality; rather, it is Othello's single act of perfect justice in the play. The cashiering of Cassio may have been the right military decision, but the act had to remain troubling to an audience that knew more than Othello at that moment; he now knows. The 'sacrifice' of Desdemona that Othello wanted to believe was a beneficial public act of justice he now knows to have been a revengeful private act of 'murder'. When he stabs himself, all the facts are in. Like the Senate speech, his last speech moves with a straightforward cadence that compels attention. As one who had made justice a principle of his life, he now asks for no mercy, just fairness: 'nothing extenuate, / Nor set down aught in malice'. And, though he acknowledges that he has 'done the state some service and they know't', he does not make that a plea for special consideration – 'No more of that' – just as he did not when he addressed the Senators back in Venice. There he was ready to lay down his life if it turned out that he did not have

Desdemona's love; here he does lay down his life because he has had it all the time and 'Like the base Indian threw a pearl away / Richer than all his tribe'. Before he begins his final speech, he asks, 'Where should Othello go?' [line 269]. Another Senate trial in Venice, such as the one held for Cinthio's Moor, would serve no purpose; for its justice cannot be so complete as Othello's upon himself, and its mercy would be meaningless to him in a world where Desdemona no longer exists. Without her the world is no longer real to him.

Both speeches, the Senate one and the last, re-enact the past in the present, but with a difference. In the earlier speech, Othello momentarily had fashioned a world of timeless perfection, based on the reality of his love, that had a genuine possibility of radiating into and energising the future. In such a perfect moment, when he greets Desdemona on Cyprus, Othello – older, more mature and experienced – cannot himself believe that such bliss can last; only Desdemona, in the eager expectation of youth, encourages him to believe otherwise [II i 177–89]. The final speech brings him back from the terrors of passion that had suddenly opened up before him to the sacredness of love. It, too, re-enacts in the present a splendid moment from the past but only to give meaning to the present, not to the future. By killing, *in narration*, the 'malignant and . . . turbaned Turk' and, *in actual fact*, the Turk that he had become, Othello unifies himself as he destroys himself, making his suicide at once surprising and inevitable. At the end he is completely without self-pity or sentimentality.

As corrupter of words in the play, Iago retreats into silence, putting himself once and for all outside the pale of humanity. Words have spelled death to Othello, but his final words restore him to the human community as he dies 'upon a kiss'. That Cassio survives Iago's machinations may be in part because he never employs words to 'fix' or dehumanise people. When Montano asks him to describe Desdemona, he replies that she 'paragons description' and 'excels the quirks of blazoning pens' [II i 62–3]; Iago is never able to undermine his devotion to his 'dear general'. If words, however, do not become 'poison' in Cassio's mouth, neither do they become the 'medicine' that helps mankind to transcend the 'shot of accident' and the 'dart of chance'. Cyprus in Cassio's governorship will be in humanly decent hands, but that hardly seems the standard, good as it is, which the play holds up as a final measure of our lives. We are left at the end with lesser people. What lingers in the mind is an image of black and white, male and female, embraced in death, that is simultaneously a vision of humanity transcending the quirks of cultural labelling and a reminder of how tragically we waste our lives and the lives of others when we cannot believe in the possibility of a love that means, as Augustine says, 'I want you to be'.

4   ANALYSIS OF SPEECHES

> O, you are well tuned now!
> But I'll set down the pegs that make this music,
> As honest as I am.   [II i 193–5]

Some years ago, G. Wilson Knight coined the phrase 'the Othello music' that has come to stand for a quality of 'exaggerated, false rhetoric' in the great speeches of Othello that makes them sound sublime but, in the last analysis, insincere. Knight found in them too much straining for effect and believed that the images were not always intrinsic to the poetry (*The Wheel of Fire*, 1930, pp. 107–31). Margaret Webster, the director of a famous production of the play, later defended the 'orchestral gamut' of Othello's poetry as necessary to convey the full heroic measure of the man in his 'passionate agony' and 'noble sorrow' (*Shakespeare Without Tears*, 1942, pp. 233–8). Othello needs this verbal music to define him; but Iago, she felt, needs 'little music' because his role, unlike Othello's, 'does not make any emotional demands upon the actor which are beyond the normal man's compass'. Ironically, just because he needs 'little music', or even lacks it, Iago seems 'well tuned now' to the prevailing anti-heroic outlook of our time. His 'alehouse' idiom, as Desdemona calls it, often sounds to the modern ear more 'honest' than Othello's 'music'. Which is, of course, what Iago would have his listeners believe!

Act I, sc. iii, lines 298–398

To talk the lovesick Roderigo out of drowning himself at the
end of the first act [iii 298–376], not out of any sympathy but
because he cannot afford to lose his 'purse', Iago begins by
selling his own image as a mature and knowing man of the
world imparting the 'gained knowledge' [line 378] of a
lifetime's experience to foolish and inexperienced youth:

> O villainous! I have looked upon the world for four times seven
> years, and since I could distinguish betwixt a benefit and an injury,
> I never found a man that knew how to love himself.

'Four times seven years', the kind of circumlocution that
advertisers enjoy, certainly sounds more impressive than a
mere 'twenty-eight years'. What Iago claims to have learned in
all those years is that the 'asses' of this world are simply those
who do not know how to look out for Number One in a
competitive society where ethical considerations, matters of
right and wrong, are nil. For Iago, the only virtues that matter
are survival and material 'benefit' to oneself. 'Put money in thy
purse', for everyone has a price, and corruptibility is the way of
the world. What the world calls romantic love is but a cover-up
for animal-like lust.

Roderigo is easy enough to fool, not only because of his youth
and inexperience or even because of the flattery that he so
obviously enjoys by being taken into the confidence of this
worldly soldier, but also because so much of what Iago says has
the ring of established truth about it. 'Put money in thy purse',
for instance, is an old proverb with none of the sordid
implications that Iago puts to it; it simply means something like
'be prepared for an emergency' and is as innocent in intent as
the proverbial 'no money, no cure'. More insidiously, in telling
Roderigo that man has been given the power of reason to
balance 'the blood and baseness of our natures', 'to cool our
raging motions, our carnal stings, our unbitted lusts', Iago is
saying nothing that any member of Shakespeare's audience
might not hear in a church sermon. That ''Tis in ourselves that
we are thus, or thus' – that we can make of ourselves rank
unweeded gardens or demi-paradises, a hell or heaven of our
lives – is good orthodox Christianity. Iago's conclusion,

however, that love is but 'a sect [cutting] or scion' of the branch
of lust does not totally convince the younger man, and rightly
so. Traditionally, reason enables man to distinguish between
love and lust. 'It cannot be', says Roderigo; but so much of
what he has just heard is accepted thinking that he cannot
figure out why not. Anyway, Iago does not give him a chance to
ponder, for he immediately expands for some twenty-six lines of
very supple prose on why love 'is merely a lust of the blood and
a permission of the will' and, therefore, why Desdemona cannot
'long continue her love to the Moor', who, like all Moors, is
'changeable' in his will. At the end of the speech, Roderigo is
totally lost and goes off to 'sell all' his land.

This dialogue between Iago and Roderigo occurs at the
tail-end of the Senate scene, and everything that has happened
before it gives the lie to Iago. Against the heaviest odds Othello
and Desdemona impress the Venetian Senators with the depth
and sincerity of their love for one another. The whole scene is a
triumph for them and for love, and Roderigo knows it. Othello
is, contrary to what Iago says, a man who *does* know 'how to
love himself' – not, of course, in Iago's self-serving sense or
egotistically as Othello's detractors claim. Othello loves himself because in his love for Desdemona, and hers for him, he has
discovered his humanity, not changed it 'with a baboon' for
'the love of a guinea-hen' (slang for 'prostitute'). Othello is
impressive because love has brought order and purpose to his
life. It is Iago, of course, who does not truly know how to love
himself, despite his bragging, and his own self-hatred fills him
with contempt and hatred for others. Iago is turned completely
inward; he soliloquises. Othello looks outward; and, until Iago
teaches him to hate himself too, he never soliloquises.

The first act ends, after the colloquy between Iago and
Roderigo, with Iago's first major soliloquy which openly
reveals his contempt for Roderigo's foolishness, his hatred for
Othello's 'free and open nature', and his envy of Cassio's
'person and . . . smooth dispose' which make him so attractive to
women. Although he has just finished praising man's faculty of
reason to Roderigo, he makes painfully clear that his hatred for
Othello goes beyond any rational explanation:

>   I hate the Moor,
> And it is thought abroad that 'twixt my sheets
> He's done my office. I know not if't be true
> But I, for mere suspicion in that kind,
> Will do as if for surety.   [i iii 380–4]

He hates Othello, whom he never personalises by name, not
'*because* it is thought . . .' or '*for* the reason it is thought . . .'; the
hatred is antecedent to motivation, but, if the world requires a
reason, he can furnish one: '*And* it is thought . . .'. Unlike
Othello later, he needs no proof of his own wife's infidelity; he
has already made clear what he thinks of all women. The
coolness of Iago's voice contrasts sharply with Othello's
passionate rage when he becomes convinced that Cassio has
done *his* office. Othello's passion will need music to express its
full force, but Iago seems almost to have no passion at all.
Besides images that connect Iago with the devil and hell, not
because he is a devil but because his mind is hell, the only other
imagery worth noting in this passage is that of pregnancy –
'womb of time', 'engendered' and 'birth', but the 'birth' is
'monstrous' and brings forth only death. In the next scene
Desdemona will speak of 'our loves and comforts [that] should
increase, / Even as our days do grow' [ii i 187–9], and Othello
responds, 'Amen to that, sweet Powers!'

Act III, sc. iii, lines 342–54

At a crucial moment in the temptation scene, just after Iago has
'a little dashed [his] spirits', and before Desdemona re-enters,
Othello ponders everything that his ensign has been saying to
him:

>   This fellow's of exceeding honesty,
>   And knows all qualities with a learnèd spirit
>   Of human dealings. . . .   [iii iii 255–7]

And yet, when Desdemona comes to call him in to dinner a few
lines later, he cannot be sure:

>   If she be false, O, then heaven mocks itself!
>   I'll not believe't.   [275–6]

Her appearance belies Iago's words, but they have by now made too deep an imprint to be dismissed out of hand. Iago's brief dialogue with Roderigo and his soliloquy that follows at the end of the first act illustrate in miniature how and why he will in the later scene successfully convince Othello of his 'exceeding honesty' and 'learnèd spirit [in] human dealings'. The earlier passage offers Iago a rehearsal for the much longer scene where convincing Othello will require more time, more subtlety, and infinitely greater care. The great depth of Othello's passion and his violent demands for proof shake Iago, and at various times he is forced to backtrack, hesitate, keep silent, and try different tacks before he achieves his goal. Roderigo is, of course, a parody of Othello; but with both men Iago employs fundamentally the same techniques, making them believe how little they know of the 'real' world, of women in particular, shaming them into thinking that they are not acting like men, and always speaking enough of the truth so that his distortions of it are not immediately apparent. He even confesses to Othello his own 'jealousy [that] Shapes faults that are not' [III iii 146–7], and in so doing confirms his 'honesty' all the more.

Towards the end of the temptation scene, after Iago has 'set' him 'on the rack', Othello delivers a speech, his 'farewell' to 'the tranquil mind' [III iii 342–54], that is frequently cited as a negative example of 'the Othello music'. In it he conjures up the full panoply of all the glorious pageantry – the 'Pride, pomp, and circumstance' – of 'the plumèd troops and the big wars / That make ambition virtue'. As if lost in a trance, he relives as much as he recalls 'the neighing steed, and the shrill trump, / The spirit-stirring drum, th'ear-piercing fife' and the 'mortal [i.e., lethal] engines, whose rude throats / Th'immortal Jove's dread clamours counterfeit'. To 'the tranquil mind' and the 'content' that he found in a soldier's life, he must now bid 'Farewell! Othello's occupation's gone'.

'Histrionic' or 'theatrical' is the most common criticism of these lines; they sound beautiful, so the argument goes, but for all their magnificence the images evoke no deeper emotion than self-pity. Even if Desdemona should prove unfaithful, why should Othello's 'occupation' as a soldier be forfeited? His love for Desdemona, it is said, could not have been all that great in the first place, for he seems to be mourning the loss of a soldier's glorious life more than the loss of Desdemona's love; he appears to be thinking more of what his fellow soldiers will say of their cuckolded general than he is of Desdemona herself, whose name he nowhere mentions. He has even been accused of substituting romantic pomp for a realistic picture of the battlefield.

Such readings, however, fail to take into account the place of this passage in the play's structure. Although many of us might have trouble finding the exact moment in this scene where the mine of his jealousy is sprung, here, as the playwright William Gibson has said, Othello takes leave of his 'psychic unity' and without question starts to become the tragic hero of the play (*Shakespeare's Game*, 1978, pp. 196–7). Not self-pity or hateful revenge, but fear that, indeed, 'Chaos is come again' animates these lines. It is true that Othello nowhere mentions Desdemona, but she is present in each of these images: for it is she, his 'fair warrior', who, by teaching him how to love himself, has made his life as a soldier meaningful. Now that world is dissolving before his eyes. The sense of order evoked by the steady piling on of the martial images, suggesting in their harmonious rhythm the serried ranks of 'the plumèd troops' themselves, is the response of a heart frightened by the sudden awareness of the emptiness of existence without love and the identity that it confers. 'Othello's occupation's gone', not because soldiers will laugh at him, but because 'Desdemona is with little exaggeration Othello's occupation' (Lawrence Danson, *The Tragic Alphabet*, 1974, p. 133). Desdemona defines his essential self and makes his 'ambition' a 'virtue' – the word as he uses it here giving the lie to Iago's shallow dismissal of it. One has to be remarkably insensitive not to hear the mourning and despair in the almost liturgical repetition of 'Farewell', six times in thirteen lines. But Iago hears no music: 'Is't possible, my lord?'

42

PART TWO: PERFORMANCE

5 INTRODUCTION

In Part Two, four stage productions have been chosen, among many, for description and comparison as contributing most usefully, in my opinion, to our understanding of key themes in *Othello* and of the range of possibility in staging and in the interpretation of character. Other productions are considered in general connection with the topics I touch on. In the Epilogue concluding Part Two I discuss film versions, and notably – as the fifth among the representative examples – the most recent one, at the time of writing.

1. Margaret Webster's 1943–44 production on Broadway; Paul Robeson as Othello, Jose Ferrer as Iago, Uta Hagen as Desdemona.

2. John Dexter's National Theatre production, London, 1964; Laurence Olivier as Othello, Frank Finlay as Iago, Maggie Smith as Desdemona.

3. John Barton's RSC production, Stratford and London, 1971–72; Brewster Mason as Othello, Emrys James as Iago, Lisa Harrow as Desdemona.

4. Peter Coe's American Shakespeare Theatre production, 1981–82; James Earl Jones as Othello, Christopher Plummer as Iago; Desdemona (in the Broadway performances) was played by Dianne Wiest and subsequently by Cecilia Hart (Mrs James Earl Jones). This production had a long pre-Broadway tour of other theatre-centres in the United States.

5. Jonathan Miller's BBC-television version, first shown in October 1981; Anthony Hopkins as Othello, Bob Hoskins as Iago, Penelope Wilton as Desdemona.

6   VARIETIES OF THEATRICAL INTERPRETATION, 1943–82

This 'most passionately human of all Shakespeare's plays' (so Micheál MacLiammóir, the Iago to Orson Welles's Othello [*Observer*, 12 April 1959]) demands in performance an articulation of its emotional line that is at every moment convincing to an audience if it is to believe in the onrush of Othello's jealousy and to be moved by his terrible misjudgement. The great speeches must come through as passion felt, not as an actor's calculated response to the lines. The failure to clarify the play's emotional movement in performance plagues modern productions, about which one reads over and over again in reviews that they suffer from 'lack of clarity' or that they lack 'any guiding principle'.

Two of this century's most famous productions, each diametrically opposed to the other in conception, had these charges levelled against them: Margaret Webster's (1943–44) with Paul Robeson as Othello and the National Theatre's (1964) with Laurence Olivier. The Royal Shakespeare Company's production of 1971–72 with Brewster Mason set out to counter the Olivier influence, but it did not escape similar censure, nor did the later (1981–82) production of the American Shakespeare Theatre with James Earl Jones. Most reviewers felt that, with the exception of the National's, these belonged aesthetically more to Iago than to Othello. We shall examine these four productions more closely. As an epilogue to this part on live stage performances, we shall also briefly examine the 1981 BBC-television *Othello* – a production in a medium which raises serious problems of its own in matters of interpretation and aesthetic balance.

From a technical viewpoint, *Othello* makes no special demands in staging. The emotions tapped in the play – love, hate, jealousy, envy – are so elemental that elaborate settings may actually detract from the bare display of them. Scene changes are likely, especially after the temptation scene [III iii], to break the momentum necessitated by the structure. On Shakespeare's empty, unlocalised stage, Venice and Cyprus reflect timeless, universal states of mind – the security conferred by civilisation, the insecurity begotten by a fortress outpost on the edge of civilisation and in a state of war – rather than actually realised places. The realism of the play lies in its emotional development, not in scenery. From what we know of contemporary staging, the first Othello probably wore typical Elizabethan garb suggesting his high office; there would have been nothing exotic (Moorish, Oriental, African) about his costume or speech. The colour of his skin alone would have been his distinguishing feature. The meticulously realistic production that Franco Zeffirelli mounted at Stratford-upon-Avon in 1961, with John Gielgud, is a cautionary example of what happens in *Othello* when excessive detail and frequent scene changes are introduced. This production, lasting almost four hours, bogged down considerably; the emotional line was almost completely obscured.

'Updating' *Othello* may bring stimulating, if limited, perspectives to the play, as was the case with the Royal Shakespeare Company's 1971–72 production, which moved the action forward to the mid-nineteenth century when British imperialism was in its fullest flowering and an Othello could assume a natural place in society as 'a brown Englishman, a servant of empire, of a kind impossible before or since Victoria' (Ronald Bryden, *Observer*, 12 September 1971). Given this setting, it did not seem surprising when Brewster Mason's Othello, a Victorian gentleman, casually stopped to light up a cheroot during his Senate speech or when Emrys James's Iago whipped out a tripod camera to photograph the wedding party upon its arrival on Cyprus. Costumes, inspired by 'Fenton's pictures from the Crimea or Matthew Brady's of the American Civil War', carefully distinguished the Venetian from the Cypriot scenes. In the former, as the programme indicated, 'The aroma of cigars and brandy infiltrates the fine cloth, gold braided jacket, and pomaded hair of the officers' whereas in the latter the military appear 'weathered and aged as their surroundings . . . coarse cloth swelling from the unwashed body and stained with its sweat. . . . The general and officers are closer to soldiers now.' Some reviewers thought that the costumes smacked a little too much of Gilbert and Sullivan, and that Desdemona in her crinolines seemed too much 'a Florence Nightingale among the Crimeans', but the careful attention to costuming made for one shocking effect: Cassio's appearance in civilian clothes after Othello has cashiered him.

The other productions sought a Renaissance look in costuming, although Robeson wore something like a Moorish caftan and Olivier a short tunic; Jones was the only one who resembled a Renaissance commander in appearance. The National Theatre (1964) and the American Shakespeare Theatre (1981–82) made good use of lighting and simple staging to keep their productions moving. In the former, a flexible use of arches and alcoves made possible a fluid transition from indoor to outdoor scenes; in the latter, hanging draperies furled and unfurled to indicate scene changes, at one point suggesting the billowing sails of a ship. The latter production also employed a freeze frame technique for Iago's soliloquies and asides: others froze while Iago spoke and a greenish (for envy?) spotlight encircled him. The Webster production of 1943–44 was divided into two acts, with four scenes each – streets, seaports, in front of a castle, inside a room in the castle, a bedroom in the castle, all of which made for a slow, lumbering production despite the heavily cut text that was used. The scenery itself looked vaguely Moorish – 'El Rancho Grande', one critic called it.

7 OTHELLO

A consensus prevails that no modern actor has played Othello to the complete satisfaction of an audience; but, since the Second World War, the performances by Paul Robeson and Laurence Olivier, however one reacted to them, stand out for the excitement and sense of discovery that each brought to the part. Robeson is the outstanding 'romantic' Othello of our time, and Olivier the outstanding 'realist'. Each exemplifies the poles of critical interpretation.

Paul Robeson's Interpretation

Robeson was not the first black actor to attempt the role. Ira
Aldridge, also an American, caused a brief flurry of interest,
mainly because of his race and his marriage to a white woman,
when his Othello appeared on the London stage in the late
nineteenth century. Critical opinion is far from unanimous over
Robeson's impact when he first took on the role in a production
at the Savoy Theatre in London in 1930, but John Dover
Wilson probably spoke for many when he later recalled, in the
introduction to his Cambridge edition of the play (1957, pp.
ix–x), that when he first saw that performance 'I felt I was
seeing the tragedy for the first time'. The real triumph for
Robeson came, however, in the 1943–44 Broadway season in
the long-running production directed by Margaret Webster.
The novelty of a black actor playing with an all-white cast for
the first time in America has to figure in any assessment of his
impact, but clearly Robeson's majestic physical stature, his
natural dignity and his grandly resonant baritone voice more
directly and emphatically account for the overwhelming
empathy that he aroused in audiences.

From his first appearance Robeson was magnificence personified, the compleat 'noble Moor'. Words like 'power',
'majesty', 'grandeur', 'sweet simplicity' and 'innocence' recur
in contemporary reviews. 'Radiant bliss' was the way that one
reviewer described his face when he was reunited with
Desdemona on Cyprus. James Earl Jones, himself a notable
Othello in later decades, recalls that 'Robeson was probably in
touch with the element of honor in a way that nobody has come
near since' (*New York Times*, 31 January 1982). Unfortunately,
Robeson was primarily a singer for the concert stage and not an
actor, and his 'romantic' Othello worked best only in the first
half of the play before destiny enmeshes him in the net of
tragedy. It seemed to many spectators that, as the play
progressed, he was never fully able to bring his Othello alive to
the overwhelming passion, the full rage and violence, that the
role also demands. From the temptation scene on, his acting
seemed 'slightly stiff', and even the 'golden voice' began to pall.
In the end, it was difficult to believe that such a monumentally
noble and trusting figure could ever be brought to murder the

wife he loved so much, and thus the murder scene lacked full credibility.

The initial impression of natural strength and dignity that Robeson brought to Othello gave rise to the much debated, though ultimately pointless, question of whether white actors should attempt the role at all. After seeing Robeson, Dover Wilson argued 'that a Negro Othello is essential to the full understanding of the play'. And Harry Levin has written that 'anyone who remembers Paul Robeson's performance is likely to be unimpressed by the voice and stature and presence of white actors playing Othello' (*Shakespeare and the Revolution of the Times*, 1976, p. 153). When in 1964 Olivier meticulously made himself up as a black man, attempting to be a genuine African and not merely a white man in blackface, Harold Clurman praised the technical feat ('notably well done') but found that 'my mind refused to acknowledge it because I could not help thinking that all this paraphernalia might be unnecessary if a Negro were acting the part' (*The Naked Image*, 1966, p. 191). For Shakespeare, who wrote the part for a white actor performing before an all-white audience, the question simply did not exist. In his time, blacks were not a subjugated people. Elizabeth I's government gave full diplomatic recognition to the Moors, who, despite their not being Christians, elicited sympathy for having conquered England's great enemy Spain in the eighth century. Iago, incidentally, whom Cinthio refers to merely as 'the Ensign', is the only Spanish name in the play. With the advent of slavery in the West and the later colonisation of Africa, audiences, particularly in England and America, became somewhat squeamish about associating Shakespeare's 'noble Moor' with the primitive (in their view) tribal black from Africa. Although Shakespeare is explicit about Othello's colour, the nineteenth century, with Edmund Kean leading the way, developed the tradition of the 'tawny' or so-called 'white' Moor. The Elizabethans themselves, for the most part, made no such distinctions between 'light' and 'dark' Moors, or between Moors and other Africans.

Today's spectator often comes to a performance of *Othello* with volatile racial concerns unknown to Shakespeare's contemporaries, and so modernity, alas, thrusts itself willy-nilly upon the play. To argue that the question of colour does not

exist at all is perverse. But it is another matter to argue that a
black actor should always act the part of Othello today or,
conversely, that only white actors are able to emphasise the
symbolic blackness of the lover as outsider, dependent on
another for his identity. If, as some believe, that the black actor
automatically reduces the full scope of the play to one only of
racial conflict, then the fault lies with that particular actor and
his director and *not* in the fact that he is black. Fundamentally,
of course, the question is finally unanswerable. In the play,
Othello *is* black whether played by a white or a black actor.
Black actors have not been notably more successful than white
ones, and the real test lies in the individual performance –
whether it works or not.

Laurence Olivier's Interpretation, 1964

At the opposite extreme from Robeson's 'noble Moor' stands
Olivier's 'realistic' egotist for the National Theatre production
of 1964, undoubtedly the most controversial portrayal of our
time. Olivier and his director, John Dexter, opted for F. R.
Leavis's view that Othello is a man in love with himself. Large
excerpts from Leavis's 1937 *Scrutiny* essay, 'Diabolic Intellect
and the Noble Hero', were reprinted, in fact, in the accompanying programme. Olivier told an interviewer at the time
that in his opinion Othello 'was only a goodish fellow who had
merely fixed the earmark of nobility upon himself' (*Life*, 1 May
1964, p. 88). But the change from the traditional Othello was
greater than that. Reviewing the film version of this production, Judith Crist wrote that instead of giving us 'the agony of
the innocent' Olivier turned Othello into 'a modern man,
riddled with neuroses, a manic-depressive skirting the edges of
paranoia' (*New York Herald Tribune*, 2 February 1966).
    Kenneth Tynan, who edited a book on the production,
reports that Dexter told his cast:

> Othello is a pompous, word-spinning, arrogant black general. . . .
> The important thing is not to accept him at his own valuation. . . .
> He isn't just a righteous man who's been wronged. He's a man too
> proud to think he could ever be capable of anything as base as
> jealousy. When he learns that he *can* be jealous, his character

1. Paul Robeson as Othello in Margaret Webster's production on Broadway, 1943–44. Photograph © Billy Rose Theatre Collection, New York Public Library at Lincoln Center.

2. The 'Temptation' scene with Othello (Paul Robeson) and Iago (Jose Ferrer) in Margaret Webster's production on Broadway, 1943–44. Photograph © Billy Rose Theatre Collection, New York Public Library at Lincoln Center.

3. John Dexter's National Theatre production, 1964, with Othello (Lawrence Olivier) and Desdemona (Maggie Smith). Photograph © Angus McBean, Harvard Theatre Collection.

4. Iago photographs the wedding party in John Barton's RSC production, 1971, at the Royal Shakespeare Theatre, with Othello (Brewster Mason) and Desdemona (Lisa Harrow). Photograph © Philip Sayers, courtesy of The Shakespeare Birthplace Trust.

5. Peter Coe's American Shakespeare Theatre production on Broadway, 1981–82, with Othello (James Earl Jones) and Iago (Christopher Plummer). Photograph © Martha Swope.

changes. The knowledge destroys him, and he goes berserk.
('Othello' by William Shakespeare: The National Theatre Production,
1966, p.4)

The advantage of such a viewpoint to a director is that it lessens the mystery of Othello and clarifies the nature of his downfall. The 'betrayal' by Desdemona becomes an affront to his ego, and his jealousy is the result of his inordinate pride, which finds an outlet in revenge. From the beginning, then, this Othello is his own tragic victim; and Iago functions only, in Leavis's words, as 'a mechanism necessary for precipitating tragedy in dramatic action' (*The Common Pursuit*, p. 141). Olivier's Othello was unquestionably at the centre of that action, and from his first entrance the actor began preparing an audience for the change that was to occur in the middle of the play.

No one who saw the production is ever likely to forget the shock of Olivier's initial appearance – not Robeson's magnificently royal Moor but, as Olivier himself described his characterisation, a 'tremendously, highly sexual' black man: kinky-haired, bare feet adorned with ankle bracelets, eyes narrowed so that just slits of white show, a short white tunic emphasising his blackness, and in his hand a crimson rose that nearly matched his sensuous red lips and tongue. Despite the huge gold crucifix that he wears, and which in the temptation scene he will savagely tear off and toss aside, this converted Othello is barely civilised, not a 'Moor of Venice' but a true African. Smug and sensually fulfilled, he obviously has just come from Desdemona and is all but indifferent to Iago's warning of Brabantio's furor. A soft-spoken baritone voice, utterly self-absorbed and self-assured, barely acknowledges the ensign's presence: ''Tis better as it is.' In the ensuing encounter with Brabantio and before the Senators in the next scene, it is clear that he does not think of himself as a member of a minority group or of an oppressed race as he aggressively flaunts his blackness, just as later he purposely will emphasise the shock of miscegenation when he embraces Desdemona. Unlike Robeson's, Olivier's Othello makes no bid for sympathy as he deliberately plays against assumptions of racial bigotry. His address to the Senators is polite enough, but a shade too flattering to be thought totally sincere. His words say one thing,

but, as Olivier utters them, they seem to point to a scarcely
disguised contempt for an effete white society and its 'curlèd
darlings'. The Senators, who need his military capability, are
not at ease. This Othello knows that he is playing a role, that he
is dramatising himself; he is in complete control.

In Othello's account of his courtship of Desdemona, Olivier
purposely eschewed 'the Othello music'. His Othello's 'words
and performances are no kin together' [IV ii 182–3] even before
Iago begins to work upon him. There is no mistaking the irony
of voice and gesture when he addresses the Senators as the
'Most potent, grave and reverend signors, / My very noble and
approved good masters' [I iii 76–7]. And when, with just the
faintest hint of sarcasm, he says, 'Her father loved me, oft
invited me' [127], Brabantio looks stunned. Throughout his
great Senate speech, Olivier's Othello never relives a courtship,
discovering or rediscovering love, but knowingly plays a game
that turns the tables by putting the Senators on trial. As Tynan
says: 'Olivier displays the public mask of Othello: a Negro
sophisticated enough to conform to the white myth about
Negroes, pretending to be simple and not above rolling his eyes,
but in fact concealing (like any other aristocrat) a highly
developed sense of racial superiority' (p. 7). Despite his words,
he lets it be known that it is not he who 'won' Desdemona, but
she him.

This new-model Othello elicited strong contradictory
responses, but just about everyone agreed in praising Olivier's
technical mastery – not only the meticulousness of his make-up
but also his total preparation for the role. Believing that this
very black Othello's speaking voice should be deeply resonant,
Olivier surprised his audiences by successfully lowering his
natural tenor voice to a baritone and by affecting what seemed
to be a West Indian accent. He also adopted a strange shuffle,
which critics compared to 'the gait of the barefooted races' but
which Olivier has claimed he stumbled upon by accident
(*Confessions of an Actor*, 1982, p. 254). Even those who keenly felt
that this was a very 'misconceived' interpretation seemed
invariably to agree with the critic John Simon that Olivier was
'always a perverse joy to behold' (*Private Screenings*, 1967, p.
211). Here was an actor taking enormous risks that only a great
actor would dare to take, and in so doing fully moving in and

occupying the role. But fascination with such audacity and
technical brilliance sometimes threatened the dramatic illusion
that the characterisation purportedly was to sustain, and some
spectators reported more awareness of Olivier's acting than of
Othello's suffering.

When all the negative criticism is registered, however, there
still remains the fact of Olivier's triumph in bringing to the part
a physical intensity and an emotional spectrum that ranged
from gentle serenity to raging madness that were missing from
Robeson and probably not seen on the English stage since the
Italian actor Tommaso Salvini performed Othello in London
in the late nineteenth century. Salvini's success was attributed in
part to his Latin temperament, thought to be more than the
English in touch with the passions aroused by sexual jealousy.
Michael Redgrave admitted as much when he declined to do
the role, feeling no empathy with it. And John Gielgud, who felt
sympathetic towards the character, inevitably over-intellec-
tualised his Othello when he undertook the part at Stratford-
upon-Avon in 1961. In chapter 24 of *Howards End*, E. M.
Forster writes that the English do not excel in the roles of
warrior, lover, or god; but Olivier's Othello proves himself a
passionate soldier and lover, and his egotism stems from his felt
superiority, not some petty foible. Tynan reports that Olivier
undertook the role with an impression that 'no English actor
ever succeeded in the part', but Olivier was never afraid to let
himself go, to pull out all the stops. Like Salvini's 'sleeping
volcano', the *Times*'s dramatic critic noted (22 April 1964),
Olivier began 'beautifully controlled' with the 'underlying
savagery' becoming 'increasingly pronounced until – in the
oath scene – he tears the cross from his neck and bows to the
floor in atavistic obeisance to a barbaric god'. His is an Othello
'easily jealous', despite his assertion to the contrary in the final
speech. To Iago's 'Ha! I like not that', when Cassio departs
from Desdemona at the beginning of the temptation scene, his
Othello immediately reacts with anger, shouting, 'What dost
thou say?' And in asking Iago, 'Was not that Cassio parted
from my wife?', he has suspicion written all over him. Here,
indeed, Iago is Leavis's mere 'mechanism'; Othello hardly
needs his provocation.

What stands out as the most surprising, even astonishing,

feature of Olivier's performance as a test case of Leavis's view of Othello is the extent to which he transcended and left behind that characterisation. At moments of greatest rage and violence, Olivier reminded his audiences of Othello's original tenderness. In the 'magic in the web' speech [III iv 55–75], in which Othello tries to impress upon Desdemona the significance of the lost handkerchief, Olivier himself noted how for weeks in rehearsal he 'intended angry insistence, but it developed into angry imploring' with which he ultimately felt more comfortable (*Life*, p. 88). And in the stark violence of the brothel scene [IV ii], even as he threw Desdemona to the floor again and again, leaving her finally in a stupor, he also wept and embraced her. This Othello was never afraid to cry. So, unexpectedly, some of 'the Othello music', in its best sense, crept back, and the sweep of the play in performance was strong enough to defy bookish interpretation. It is safe to say that no modern production has left such a lasting impression of the final moments of the play: as he started his last speech, Olivier's Othello lifted the white-clad body of Desdemona and completely enfolded her within the circle of his fully exposed black arms, rocking back and forth with her until the moment that he slipped a small dagger from his bracelet and, still defiant, stabbed himself. In no way could this Othello be said to be 'cheering himself up'. The 'romantic' sympathy that Olivier set out to counter somehow subsumed the 'realistic' Othello.

The unexpected combination of 'realism' and 'romanticism', coupled with the bravura of his acting, that made Olivier the most debated and 'the most technically interesting Othello of our time' (Henry Hewes, *Saturday Review*, 30 May 1964), was bound to have a stimulating effect on other actors, but one reviewer of a later anti-heroic Othello worried – and he was not alone – that 'Sir Laurence will have a lot to answer for if his Calypso Othello leads to a succession of other actors' seeing the main challenge as one of impersonation' (Peter D. Smith, *Shakespeare Quarterly*, 17, 1966, p. 414).

Brewster Mason's Interpretation, 1971–72

When Brewster Mason undertook the role for the Royal

Shakespeare Company's production in 1971, the first since
Olivier's, Othello's normal challenge to an actor was that much
greater. Nevertheless, Mason and director John Barton went a
long way 'to rescue the play from spending a generation pinned
under Olivier's interpretation, showing that no one reading can
exhaust it' (Ronald Bryden, *Observer*, 12 September 1971). In
his highly favourable review, Bryden made the astute observation that Mason's Othello was 'a Moor for the seventies' – 'a
more hopeful decade, which recognises how much "aggression" is simply defensiveness, and believes it may overcome by
love'. In contrast, Olivier's Moor now seemed, in retrospect, 'a
sixties Othello, born of the decade which discovered Black
Power, ethology and animal aggression'.

An untamed barbarian, always ready to explode, lurked
beneath Olivier's surface; Mason eschewed completely the
slightest hint of the primitive, his 'blackness' denoting not
something racial but a larger and more uncomprehending
alienation to which all of us, of any race, might respond. To
Iago's insinuating query early in the temptation scene –

Did Michael Cassio
When you wooed my lady, know of your love? [III iii 93–4]

– Olivier's Othello, making perfectly clear his own self-
conscious awareness of what Iago was getting at, responded
with instant anger: 'He did, from first to last. Why dost thou
ask?' To the same query, however, Mason's Othello registered
complete surprise; and, from this point until the end, as Iago's
innuendoes gave way to concrete particulars in his own mind,
he seemed more stunned by what was happening to him than
jealous or angry. The dramatic critic for the *Leicester Mercury* (10
September 1971) noted that Mason went 'about his grim
business with almost hypnotic purpose', so that even when
Desdemona pleaded for her life, 'her beauty and her sweet,
innocent face' provoked 'no tormenting uncertainty' in him. By
the brothel scene [IV ii], Olivier in his feral madness had
reached a point of no return; the murder of Desdemona was
already inevitable. Brewster Mason, however, in this same
scene, was able to effect a rather unexpected tension because
his supremely trusting and gentle portrayal made it momentarily possible to hope that reconciliation with Desdemona

might still come about. Its failure to materialise was that much
sadder. Furthermore, as reviewers observed, Mason's return to
the more traditional Othello, serene and slow to jealousy, made
his striking of Desdemona [IV i 240] all the more shocking
because it was so completely out of character. The nobly
rendered final speech did not so much restore dignity to a fallen
hero as clarify what was there the whole time.

Praiseworthy and less controversial as this Othello was, even
those critics who were not reconciled to Olivier's 'African'
interpretation reflected the impact that it undoubtedly had
made upon them. Much as they found to admire in Mason's
'low key' performance, many felt, as Felix Barker did, that he
'appeared to be holding himself in', that 'he simply declined to
be swept away on the turbulent tide of passion that the role
demands' (*Evening News*, 9 September 1971). Like Robeson,
Mason proved not to be caught up by the structure of the play
and thus was unable to fully negotiate the transition from the
romantic and heroic Othello of the first half of the play to the
agonising and tragic Othello of the second half. The performance commanded the pathos but not the fiercer terror, and
grandeur, of tragedy. Mason's gentler qualities mostly worked
against him in the central portion of the play where, to some
viewers, he now appeared 'something of a simpleton', too naïve
and innocent, Iago's 'dupe' rather than victim (David Isaacs,
Evening Telegraph, Coventry, 10 September 1971). The rich
timbre of Mason's voice, so moving in the Senate scene and at
the reunion on Cyprus, tended to become a shade monotonous.
B. A. Young echoed others when he wrote that Mason's 'deep,
resonant tones vary little between "she loved me" ' of the
Senate speech and the 'farewell' to his occupation midway
through the temptation scene: 'They all come out slow, silky,
self-contented and void of any genuine emotion' (*Financial
Times*, 10 September 1971). Reviewing the play after it had
moved from Stratford-upon-Avon to London during the following summer, Garry O'Connor made the interesting observation that the 'great intelligence' that Mason applied to the
lines made it seem as if he succeeded in proving 'to himself that
Desdemona has been unfaithful to him, and ultimately he looks
more like a fool than one temporarily possessed and mad with
jealousy' (*Financial Times*, 19 July 1972). What should have

been experienced as an onrush of jealousy seemed like a more calculated response. 'Where should Othello go?' [v ii 269]. Mason's 'Moor for the seventies', admirable in so many ways, had no need to ask this tragic question, for ultimately he did not seem rent by any tragic division in his soul.

James Earl Jones's Interpretation, 1981–82

The Othello that James Earl Jones brought to Broadway in February 1982, after a long tour of the United States, was bound to revive memories of Robeson's triumph in 1943. Both actors create magnificent physical presences on stage, and each has a deep, almost cavernous voice that can be very stirring – Jones, in fact, doing his Darth Vader voice from *Star Wars*. Jones admittedly surpasses Robeson as an actor, but, because he chose to underplay the role (possibly to contrast with Robeson's monumentally noble Moor and Olivier's eye-rolling African), his impact was not so great. Rightly understanding how Iago's kind of stereotyping violates Othello's character, Jones dismissed a racial interpretation of the part ('more sociological than psychological'), and in an interview he claimed that 'all the attempts to define Othello are really ways to dismiss him' (*New York Times*, 31 January 1982). In this, his sixth attempt in the role, Jones opted for a gentle, very humane, and even at times 'childlike' Othello: not a role model for blacks but an 'oddly vulnerable' human being despite his initial ease and authority in a strange environment. In the first half of the play, underplaying worked to his advantage: his gentleness and modesty and almost fatherly affection for Desdemona lent him strength and dignity. And yet, when it became necessary, he cashiered Cassio with believable, almost frightening, military authority.

But from the temptation scene until the end of the play, the impressive underplaying of the first half worked against Jones, tending to lessen the credibility of his characterisation and to slow down what should have been the onrush of destruction that the structure of the play calls for. His Othello, finally, was just too much of a piece, with no appreciable build-up from his initial serenity to anything like the shattering madness that should have engulfed him. However negatively one may have reacted to Olivier's interpretation, it did manage to touch that core of passion; that actor was not afraid to go insane. William Gaskill has commented on how, 'when he took that line "Farewell the tranquil mind" ' [III iii 345], Olivier 'delivered it in a totally original way': 'It may have been the wrong interpretation, but it was very effective. As you know, it's usually done as a sad, reflective, contemplative speech, but he did it on a note of attacking frenzy, which was bold and arresting' (in *Olivier*, ed. Logan Gourlay, 1974, p. 173). Jones, unfortunately, was not so much 'reflective' or 'contemplative' as divorced from the lines; speaking in almost a monotone, he conveyed no sense of what he had really lost. And without that sense of loss, there can be little sense of tragedy.

Strangely enough, although he never intended to separate words from performance, as Olivier distinctly had, Jones sometimes appeared alienated from what he was saying. In the Senate speech, where his interpretation was diametrically opposed to Olivier's, Jones likewise failed to communicate that he was reliving an experience in which he was discovering love for the first time. Olivier, however, was consciously playing with that speech; Jones was not. And Jones's gentle portrayal, though it worked well early on, failed to clarify his relationship to Desdemona in a way that Brewster Mason's tenderness in the Royal Shakespeare Company production had not; its ultimate effect was to make the murder scene seem dispassionate. One reviewer described Jones's delivery of the final speech 'as if the character had prepared it in advance and was dictating it to a stenographer to be distributed at an upcoming press conference' (Ernest Albrecht, *The Home News*, New Brunswick, N.J., 5 February 1982). Gestures, as well as speeches, also seemed studied – as his obscene phallic gestures in crying out 'Goats and monkeys!' before Lodovico [IV i 265] or his slashing of Iago's genitals in the final scene. Such gestures, rather than emphasising Othello's descent into Iago's world of lunacy, made him appear merely vulgar and were certainly not prepared for by the earlier portrayal. In general, Jones's failure to communicate deep passion made for a slow-moving production.

What is most ironic is that, because of his self-conscious use

of language and gesture, something of a Leavisite self-
dramatising characterisation crept into Jones's performance
only to mar it; whereas Olivier, maybe because of his long
experience in classical theatre and with dramatic verse, seemed
to go beyond this intended interpretation. With Olivier, the
eloquence returned from time to time, as if demanded by the
Shakespearean line; but Jones seemed to have no grasp of
Shakespearean melody. Most spectators may not know what
blank verse is, and those who do certainly do not expect an
actor to singsong the da-dum da-dum of an iambic line. But
failure to take into account the natural accents of Shakespearean verse is liable to create a tension within the listening
audience that may lead finally to boredom.

Henry James wrote of Salvini's Othello: 'No more complete
picture of passion can have been given to the stage in our day, –
passion beginning in noble repose and spending itself in black
insanity.' But he also noted that 'Certain exquisite things are
absent from it, – the gradations and transitions which Shakespeare had marked in a hundred places, the manly melancholy,
the note of deep reflection, which is sounded as well as the note
of passion' (in *The Atlantic Monthly*, March 1883; reprinted in
The Scenic Art, ed. Allan Wade, 1948, p. 173). The full 'Othello
music' requires both notes.

8   Iago

He that plays the villain cannot be blamed entirely if, without
meaning to, he steals the show. The balance between the earlier
heroic and the later tragic Othello that is so difficult for an actor
to strike has no counterpart in Iago's role. Like Falstaff's,
Iago's versatility in role-playing also gives him innate advan-
tages over the other characters in the play. In the last century
Edwin Booth played both Othello and Iago, sometimes
interchangeably in the same season, but with Iago he found
greater success. Of the Othellos we have looked at – Robeson,
Olivier, Mason, and Jones – only Olivier can be said to have

fully maintained the title character's dominance although at some cost to interpretation.

Jose Ferrer's Interpretation, 1943–44

Robeson made an indelible impression upon those who saw him in the Margaret Webster production on Broadway, 1943–44, but a number of reviewers at the time felt that the play belonged aesthetically to Jose Ferrer's Iago. Mary McCarthy, for one, admitted that Robeson appeared 'magnificent' in the early scenes where 'he is not over-taxed by the character', but 'unfortunately, [he] is not an actor' (*Sights and Spectacles*, 1956, pp. 73–4). What she is saying, of course, is that Robeson was unable to negotiate the subtle change from epic romance to tragedy. 'It is Jose Ferrer's Iago that is the star-piece of this production', she added, particularly admiring the way that he established the 'division of Iago's nature between the man as good fellow and the man as destroyer'.

Some reviewers thought that Robeson was 'over-awed' by Ferrer's seemingly effortless acting style, but Ferrer was the one who admitted to being overawed: 'To have to play an entire evening against a voice of that magnitude is apt to be a terrifying experience at first', he later wrote ('The Role of Iago in Shakespeare's *Othello*', *Notes on the American Theatre*, I, August 1945, p. 8). Luckily, for building his own confidence, he discovered that the abundant humour in Iago's part that distinguished him from the other characters gave him a handle on the role. A critic reviewing a later Iago recalled, in comparison, the 'positively sensual' delight that Ferrer's Iago took in 'his own nastiness' (Arthur Sainer, *Village Voice*, 22 October 1964). Ferrer's fondling of the lieutenant's sash that Cassio had thrown to the ground after his dismissal was, indeed, 'positively sensual'.

To his credit, Ferrer never tried to upstage Robeson or to dominate the production. He believed that if he made his villainy believable Othello would never appear gullible, and in this he was largely successful. 'I have to manage to suggest a very careful, frank, open love and dependability about the man', he wrote; and he was able to do so by always playing 'the simplest, most trustworthy character I could suggest when in the presence' of others. Only in the soliloquies did Iago's true maliciousness assert itself openly; but, as Ferrer saw, 'only the lightest touch' was necessary 'to make the soliloquy scenes the embodiment of evil'. Neither Ferrer nor Webster worried about Iago's motivation but relied on the brilliance of his performance to make the character convincing.

In contrast to the 'bully sergeant' lower-class portrayal of Iago in vogue these days, Ferrer's ensign was truly of officer class. Young, handsome, dashing, Ferrer moved about the stage with a dancer's grace – 'as if choreographed by Balanchine' (Sainer). Marvin Rosenberg has described Ferrer as being 'brilliant, powerful – and wrong', too 'clever' in the part (*The Masks of Othello*, 1961, p. 157). But most reviewers admired his 'great variety' and 'flexible power', his ability to be, in turn, charming, humorous, cruel, arrogant, coldly intellectual, cynical, and fearful, as in the temptation scene when he starts to run away in fright from the threatening Othello ('Take note, take note . . .' [III iii 374]), but then runs back and embraces his general over whom he now has gained the upper hand.

As an artist enjoying what he has wrought, Ferrer's Iago provided the only aesthetic variety in the Webster production.

Frank Finlay's Interpretation, 1964

Altogether different was Frank Finlay's Iago in the National Theatre production of 1964. Here it was Olivier's Othello who played the artist, serenely conscious of his success before Brabantio and the Venetian Senators and later passionately, even savagely, conscious of his increasing loss of self-control. Though meant negatively, the headline over *The Times*'s review (22 April 1964), 'The Moor Built up at Iago's Expense', confirms the success of Olivier and his director, John Dexter, in their determination to make the play belong unequivocally to Othello. It is an astonishing headline, if one stops to think about it, in the history of *Othello* performances. The writer of the review describes Finlay's Iago as a 'lumpish figure' with 'a plodding sameness' – none of the 'speed, changeable resourcefulness, nimble invention' that could be said to have characterised Ferrer's portrayal – and concludes that 'Othello needs an adversary, not an accomplice'.

But Dexter and Olivier were engaged in a bold experiment of testing by actual performance F. R. Leavis's anti-heroic – or, as Leavis preferred, 'realistic' – conception of Othello as a role-playing self-deceiver who ultimately needs no outside force to destroy him. Iago, therefore, serves purely, in Leavis's words, in a 'subordinate and merely ancillary role' as just a device to precipitate the tragedy. To Robeson's highly romantic and conventionally heroic general, Ferrer played a villain who, in the joy of performance, transcended ordinary questions of motivation. In contrast, Finlay's Iago had no joy in him at all; his laughter was mordant, his humour sick. His motivations were all too clear: failure to get ahead, racial prejudice, class envy, sexual frustration and impotency. No mystery adhered to this Iago, described in reviews as a 'redneck', 'less a Machiavell than one of those amoeba-minded Southern Senators', an 'hysterical small-town segregationalist, who was not always believable', 'more . . . of a groom or stableboy to Othello, than ensign'.

In the interview that he gave to *Life* magazine at the time, Olivier admitted that he wanted opposite him an Iago who was not 'the cunning, Renaissance villain' but 'the noncommissioned officer type' – 'a stolid sort you would not suspect of such guile, so Othello does not look so absurdly gullible and unbelievable and untragic to a modern audience'. Where Ferrer played a Venetian among Venetians, Finlay, like Olivier's Othello, was the complete outsider. Among the elegantly attired upper-class 'curlèd darlings' he sported a cropped head of hair and dressed simply in a plain military leather tunic studded with metal to suggest the mail armour of a soldier. Instead of relishing the rhythms of Shakespearean verse on his tongue, Finlay affected a provincial north country accent, muttering sometimes so that he seemed hard to hear; and his blunt, streetwise delivery gave plausibility to the 'honesty' that others saw in him. Frustrated by his failure to rise in the ranks and to overcome class distinctions, he could barely hide his contempt for Roderigo, over whom he assumed an easy power; but alongside his general the ensign appeared a very small man indeed, 'flimsy' as *The Times*' dramatic critic wrote. What made Iago's bitterness especially believable was the success of a man like Cassio – played, somewhat contrary to the text (by Derek Jacobi), not as a possible rival for Desdemona's affections or as a potential governor of Cyprus, but as an effeminate dandy of the upper classes: so clearly a lightweight that only the unfairness of life itself could have advanced him above Iago.

Finlay's dark, brooding intensity constantly bespoke a younger man's streak of ruthlessness that signalled not only hatred for others but also hatred for himself as a man left out of the 'daily beauty' of life that others enjoyed without questioning. The unsympathetic realism of his portrayal made him appear brutally intellectual to many viewers, but the truth is that, as the play moved along, he looked almost mentally unstable, so frustrated by failure that he was ready to wreak vengeance on the nearest available victim. Nowhere did the corrosive inner rage of this Iago reveal itself more than in the pervasive but inhibited sexuality that surrounded his characterisation. Tynan reports that 'in Frank Finlay's interpretation, endorsed by Dexter, Iago has been impotent for years – hence his loathing of Othello's sexuality and his alienation from Emilia' (p. 8). This Iago cannot tolerate Emilia's hands on him, although he often takes Roderigo's hand in his. Given to lewd gestures – can one ever forget the way that Finlay wiggled his finger as he informed Roderigo what 'th'incorporate conclusion' inevitably must be between Cassio and Desdemona [II i 254]? – and obsessed with sexual longings that he apparently cannot fulfill, he is strangely drawn to those whom he envies and hates. Towards the strong black man whose virility he cannot imitate, his ambivalence is unforgettably clarified when, after Othello breaks down and 'falls' to the ground in a trance [IV i 42 ff.], Iago straddles him and thrusts the handle of his dagger into his victim's mouth. Shortly afterwards, when the arrival of Lodovico is announced, Iago wipes the spittle from Othello's tongue.

A number of reviewers thought that Finlay was 'miscast' in the role. Finlay, wrote Alan Dent, 'makes a furtive slyboots of the character, and this makes nonsense of Othello's regard for him, of his own wife's loyalty, and of the complete trust placed in him by everybody else' (quoted in Tynan, p. 102). Writing of

Finlay's 'utter unsuitability for the role of Iago', Harold Clurman judged the portrayal 'a trick to heighten the effect of an effulgent Othello by a dun Iago' (*The Naked Image*, 1966, p. 192). How could any Othello have been taken in by such a character? The answer is, Olivier's Othello was not – an interpretation sanctioned by Leavis: 'It is plain that what we should see in Iago's prompt success is not so much Iago's diabolic intellect as Othello's readiness to respond . . . the essential traitor is within the gates' (pp. 140–1).

The essential traitor was back outside the gates, however, when in 1971–2 Emrys James's loutish Iago overshadowed Brewster Mason's gentle, subdued Othello at Stratford-upon-Avon and in London; and again, ten years later, when Christopher Plummer played the devilish ensign to James Earl Jones's vulnerably human Moor. Both Iagos were totally different in conception, but they ran away with their productions because their respective Othellos were finally unable to plumb the inner depths of the tragedy. Like Robeson's, Mason's and Jones's largely monochromatic performances were no match for the vividly realised Iagos who opposed them. James and Plummer developed their parts with such high spirits that they threw the emotional balance of both productions out of kilter.

Emrys James's Interpretation, 1971–72

James's Iago owed much, on the surface at least, to Finlay's lower-class, envy-gnawed soldier from the provinces. He, too, affected a provincial accent (a flat North Midland in this case), dressed plainly, and among the 'curlèd darlings' of Venice went even further than his predecessor – this Iago was bald headed! Totally lewd and vulgar, he also resembled Finlay in being a little man – in this case, at least a head smaller than Mason. And the motivations that prompted him were, like Finlay's, clearly spelled out. His hatred and revenge were directed squarely 'against those who control society and so control his destiny' (Dàvid Isaacs, *Evening Telegraph*, Coventry, 10 September 1971). A mess sergeant Iago, yes, but definitely not 'officer material' (Ian Christie, *Daily Express*, 10 September 1971).

But where Finlay was a 'dun Iago' to an 'effulgent Othello', just the reverse was true here, justifying the description of the play as director John Barton's 'tragi-comedy of Iago' (Frank Marcus, *Sunday Telegraph*, 12 September 1971). Up against this outwardly genial, exuberant, concertina-playing joker of the barracks room, 'a rather likeable rogue' ('D.D.', *Leicester Mercury*, 10 September 1971), Mason's supremely gentle Moor – 'like some kindly Negro nanny' (Marcus) – had no chance; for most of the performance, he was putty in his ensign's hands. Enjoying a good laugh almost from the start, James's giggling vulgarian cackled even over the dead bodies in the final moments of the play, and so did some of the audience. Finlay may have seemed demented at times, but this Iago turned out to be a psychopath, absolutely insane. Ronald Bryden found this 'resourceful, ingratiating and shameless' portrayal of Iago 'the most credible' he had seen (*Observer*, 12 September 1971), and Felix Barker deemed this 'quite revolting mixture of hollow bonhomie and perverted villainy' as 'the best Iago of this generation' (*Evening News*, 9 September 1971).

But, in subordinating Othello to Iago, the Royal Shakespeare Company subordinated tragedy to comedy, creating 'less of a supreme tragedy than a moving record of a stratagem practised by an evil spirit upon a trusting, loving soul' (J. C. Trewin, *Birmingham Post*, 10 September 1971).

Christopher Plummer's Interpretation, 1981–82

Nor was it 'supreme tragedy' that James Earl Jones and Christopher Plummer brought to New York in 1981–82, after a lengthy pre-Broadway tour. A 'near-comic tragedy' is, in fact, how one reviewer described a production that veered constantly towards old-fashioned Victorian melodrama (Peter Wynne, *Record*, 4 February 1982). Audiences laughed (in delight, it seems) when they should have been gasping or struck silent with horror, and they hissed and booed the villain much as if they had been watching the wicked schoolmaster Squeers in *Nicholas Nickleby*. The mere repetition of '*honest* Iago' was often enough to evoke laughter. Charles Michener of *Newsweek* (14 February 1982) reports how 'On opening night the audience burst into applause in the last scene when Plummer was dragged back in to face the music. The applause was as much for the return of his spellbinding presence as it was for the villain caught.' Thus, at the moment when it should have been most keenly felt, the fullest impact of Othello's tragedy was nullified. Two opposed acting styles – Jones's underplaying of Othello and Plummer's overplaying of Iago – worked against the subtlety of Shakespearean tragedy, transforming the play into the more obvious opposition of Evil to Innocence, with Evil holding the upper hand from the beginning. Eliminated entirely was that element of danger so necessary to creating tension in the temptation scene. *Newsweek* frankly proclaimed that the play 'should be retitled "Iago"' and the production convinced Robert Brustein, drama critic for the *New Republic*, 'that Iago is the true author of Othello's play' (10 March 1982).

Plummer's Iago was a far cry from the provincial, class-conscious portrayals by Finlay or James, even though he, too, sported a cropped head of hair and dressed in unpretentious military garb, even down to his scuffed boots. The resemblance was closer to Ferrer's Iago – definitely of officer rank, not lower class, and whose hatred and thirst for revenge far transcended ordinary questions of motivation. Significantly, Iago's reference to Cassio's 'daily beauty' [v i 19] was cut. Lean, trim, agile, like Ferrer, Plummer moved about the stage as if he, too, had been choreographed – but as a reptile. The contrast with the ponderousness of Jones was all too obvious. There were some hints of homosexuality in the portrayal, but Frank Rich was probably more on the mark in seeing Plummer as 'a sexless Iago who playfully kisses men and women alike because he has no use for either' (*New York Times*, 4 February 1982). The vulgarity that Finlay and James brought to the part was largely absent.

Ferrer had tried to subordinate himself to Robeson, but Plummer admitted to an interviewer that he saw Iago's and Othello's roles as equals:

> Whenever I've seen the play, it has been overbalanced to Othello or to Iago, edited down either way. . . . I feel Shakespeare wrote two big performances, and I insisted most of it stay in. I wanted to give a rather daring and huge performance. Othello is on a grand scale, and I am positive Iago is meant to be, too. He's not just a little jealous man who envies Othello, seeks power, can't get it and

decided to topple the world. I'm sure Shakespeare wanted him to be thought of as a huge, timeless creature possessed by the devil or by other powers over which he has no control. Whether anybody agrees with me or not, that's the performance I try to give.

(*New York Times*, 9 March 1982)

Petty spite motivated Finlay and James, but Plummer's hatred was monumental, more so even than Ferrer's. Where Ferrer, however, brought an element of good humour to the role, Plummer personified evil with no trace of warmth to his soul at all. Looking a bit like one of Eliot's 'hollow men', no longer young, hair graying, face ashen, voice dry, and with a kind of weariness overtaking him in his soliloquies when he was not role-playing before others, he seemed at times his own worst victim. Victory over someone as innocent and gullible as Jones's Othello was too easy to be pleasureable.

Reviewers reacted to Plummer much as they had to Olivier: some were unstinting in their admiration, but even those who thought that his self-indulgent theatricalism made a shambles of the play that Shakespeare wrote could not help but admire his artistry, his technical virtuosity. Walter Kerr reflected the former attitude: 'It is quite possibly the best single Shakespearean performance to have originated on this continent in our time. . . . Mr. Plummer so enjoys playing the consummate hypocrite that one comes not only to admire but even to *like* this Iago for his extraordinary gifts.' Kerr saw in Plummer's Iago a 'born loser' who uses his 'despair as a source of energy': 'The concept is brilliant, the execution of it perfect' (*Sunday New York Times*, 14 February 1982). Other reviewers, like Vineta Colby, were more clearly disturbed: 'Every movement is arresting, but the total impression is wrong because it turns Iago into a monstrous satanic presence. The horror of his evil is not that it is natural, banal, conscienceless, and part of the reality of the world in which we live' (*Park East*, February 1982). The reviewer for the *Philadelphia Inquirer* simply confessed to the 'perverse pleasure' that he took in watching Plummer's Iago, like watching 'a skillfully dirty hockey player' (William B. Collins, 4 February 1982). Critics earlier had noticed how Finlay's 'dun Iago' sometimes seemed lost on the stage of the National Theatre, but Plummer's 'effulgent' Iago made the vast stage of Broadway's Winter Garden Theatre 'sometimes seem too small' (Glenne Currie, United Press release, 10 February 1982).

We cannot be sure how Iago was played in Shakespeare's day. Possibly he, too, was hissed and booed as a Machiavellian villain. But there seems no doubt that Richard Burbage's Othello, remembered and praised long after his death, was not too small for the Globe stage. We do not know who his Iago was.

9 DESDEMONA

If an overpowering Iago makes a shambles of the play that Shakespeare wrote, so does a feckless Desdemona. Altogether too many productions focus on the Othello–Iago rather than on the more significant Othello–Desdemona relationship, which is, after all, at the heart of the tragedy. Othello assumes at first that with 'proof' of Desdemona's infidelity, 'there is no more but this: / Away at once with love or jealousy!' [III iii 189–90]. That is melodrama. Tragedy comes to Othello when he understands clearly that he has no simple choice, for in Desdemona, as he says:

> . . .   I have garnered up my heart,
> Where either I must live, or bear no life,
> The fountain from the which my current runs,
> Or else dries up . . .   [IV ii 56–9]

To Desdemona a choice is incomprehensible; her love is absolute:

> . . .   Unkindness may do much,
> And his unkindness may defeat my life,
> But never taint my love. . . .   [IV ii 158–60]

His 'unkindness' does defeat her life, and his too. Their bond of love is their undoing, but in the end it proves stronger than all of Iago's hate. The impression of their wasted lives should haunt an audience more than the spell of Iago's 'humour' or Machiavellian cleverness. For this to happen, an audience must see in Othello what Desdemona sees in him, his 'visage in his mind'; but, equally, it must see in Desdemona what he sees in her, 'so lovely fair' and one who compels him to be 'free and bounteous to her mind'. A complete humanity, physical and spiritual, unites them. 'Let me go with him', she pleads to the Senators. His ultimate accolade to her is simply: 'my fair warrior'.

With few exceptions, in the many productions in which the Iagos dominate, the Desdemonas prove, as often as their Othellos, unexceptional. Iago's role is so actor-proof that it is probably impossible for an actor to 'ham' up the part too much. But to turn innocence and uncomprehending suffering into an active and convincing stage presence offers a tremendous challenge to an actress today. Robert Brustein makes an interesting observation along these lines: 'the passive, virtuous, all-suffering Desdemona is a part that must be inhabited rather than impersonated – which may be why it is so difficult to cast in an age of women's liberation' (*New Republic*, 10 March 1982). Few actresses are able to balance child-like innocence and mature womanhood in a rounded characterisation; too often they seem either childish or so worldly intelligent that it is inconceivable that they would land themselves in this mess.

Uta Hagen's Interpretation, 1943–44

Whether the play belonged to Paul Robeson's Othello or to Jose Ferrer's Iago in the Margaret Webster production is still a subject of debate, but in that debate Uta Hagen's (Mrs Ferrer's) Desdemona figures not at all. Reviews at the time mention her in passing, but she seems to have made no impression one way or another. One reviewer summed up the prevailing attitude when he wrote that he 'could take her or leave her' (Robert Garland, *New York Journal American*, 25 May 1945).

The fault may not have been entirely Hagen's; for Webster's promptbook, now in the New York Library of the Performing Arts, indicates that the part, not all that large to begin with, was sufficiently 'cleaned up' so that only the child-like innocence of the character remained. Her banter with Iago at

the beginning of the second act, before Othello arrives at
Cyprus, is severely cut, including her sophisticated reference to
Iago's 'alehouse humour'. Her declaration to Iago later, 'I
cannot say "whore" ' [iv ii 160] is also omitted, Webster not
allowing her to say even that much! Also deleted is a major
portion of the passage in which she blames herself for Othello's
unhappy state [iii iv 136–50]. Iago's reference to her as being
'framed as fruitful / As the free elements' [ii iii 331–2] and
Othello's, though not Iago's, to her being 'naked in bed' [iv i
4–8] have been cut. Hagen apparently, according to the
promptbook, put up a struggle on her deathbed, but the overall
impression is of a 'nice' girl, with nothing of the 'fair warrior'
about her. One strange bit of stage business ought perhaps to
be mentioned: at the beginning of the temptation scene, when
Cassio first comes to Desdemona to ask her to plead his suit
with Othello, they drink mutual toasts to one another.
Desdemona as perfect hostess?

Dianne Wiest's Interpretation, 1982

'Drawling like an anxious debutante hostess trying to enliven a
dreary cocktail party' is, in fact, how one reviewer described
Dianne Wiest's Desdemona opposite James Earl Jones's
Othello in the Broadway opening of the American Shakespeare
Festival production (Stephen Harvey, *SoHo News*, 10 February
1982). He went on to say, 'she delivers a bitchy parody of frail
feminine rectitude'. One or two reviewers did find Wiest
'appealing' and 'tender', but most thought that the actress,
normally strong in other roles, was 'miscast' or 'a major
handicap'.
    From the beginning, when it opened in Connecticut the
preceding summer, and throughout its lengthy pre-Broadway
tour, the production ran afoul of its Desdemonas; Wiest was the
third. The first Desdemona was described as 'looking like a
vapid starlet on the beach at Malibu' (John Simon, *New York*, 7
September 1981), and a Chicago reviewer described the
touring Desdemona as 'a corpse from the first scene' (Bury St
Edmund, *Reader*, 27 November 1981). Only in the last few
weeks of the Broadway run was a more convincing actress,

Cecilia Hart (Mrs James Earl Jones) brought in, but by then the production had run its course. The major criticism of Wiest, as of her predecessors, was sheer inability to make Shakespearean verse come alive with feeling. Inevitably, an unbridgeable distance opened up between actress and audience, as well as, it seemed, between her and Othello, which may partially account for what was felt to be Jones's unfelt involvement with her. Their marriage seemed implausible and the murder scene may well have been 'the most dispassionate murder of passion in stage history' (Stewart Klein, for WNEW-TV, New York, 3 February 1982).

'I am a child to chiding', says Desdemona [IV ii 113], and Wiest seems to have taken, or had been directed to take, the reference to the 'child' Desdemona too literally, as when, in the brothel scene [IV ii], after Othello's unexpectedly harsh treatment of her, she curled up on stage in a near-foetal position. At odd moments she affected a disconcerting little-girl giggle. Wiest's Desdemona was also something of a tease: at the beginning of the temptation scene, she entered carrying a rose, with which she jabbed Othello on the head and then coyly threw it to him. Klein rightly observed that 'this is not Shakespearean innocence but Rebecca of Sunnybrook Farm'. Moments like these gave the impression that every movement was calculated, not felt – in Brustein's words, 'impersonated', not 'inhabited'. Frank Rich pointed out that 'in the slapping scene [IV i], her sorrow . . . seems a bit second-hand': 'If there's not a flowing, open-hearted Desdemona to balance Iago, an Othello can't easily dramatize the hero's violent swings between the author's poles of good and evil' (*New York Times*, 4 February 1982). A Desdemona who is neither 'fair warrior' nor one for whom 'the sense aches' creates a vacuum at the centre of the tragedy which the liveliness of Iago rushes in to fill.

Lisa Harrow's Interpretation, 1971–72

Youth and innocence need not mean mindlessness or foolishness as Lisa Harrow had made clear in her touchingly convincing portrayal of Desdemona to Brewster Mason's Othello for the Royal Shakespeare Company in the Strat-

ford–London seasons of 1971–2. Playing the part with a
'child-like fragility' that Gareth Lloyd Evans, among others,
found 'intensely affecting' (*Guardian*, 10 September 1971),
Harrow added an unusual and interesting variation to this
traditional interpretation. Remaining completely innocent
herself, she nevertheless managed to impart 'an ambiguous
sensuous possibility' to the role (so Garry O'Connor, *Financial
Times*, 19 July 1972). Although neither Mason nor Harrow
brought any sense of a deep sexual passion to their relationship,
Harrow's characterisation 'for once', as Michael Billington,
writing of the London performance, indicated, 'makes
Othello's suspicions seem vaguely plausible' (*Guardian*, 19 July
1972). Ian Christie said much the same thing about the earlier
Stratford performance: 'Judging by the way Desdemona and
Cassio flirt with each other, I am by no means certain that
Othello's suspicions were unfounded' (*Daily Express*, 10 September 1971). Of course, all this makes Iago's accusations
'vaguely plausible' also; an audience rarely has this chance to
see how 'evidence' from multi-sided characterisation works in
Othello.

Furthermore, this double-edged portrayal by Harrow pointed up more directly than, say, the Jones–Wiest performances,
the vulnerability at the heart of this marriage of an older man,
of different race and culture, to a younger woman. On Othello's
telling her about the 'magic in the web' of the lost handkerchief,
Harrow's Desdemona was so innocent and guileless that she
registered neither fear nor shock at first. At the mention of the
'sibyl, that had numbered in the world / The sun to course two
hundred compasses' [iii iv 70–1], she broke into a giggle, and
the tone and manner of her response – 'Then would to God that
I had never seen it! – clearly indicated that she regarded his
telling her this tale as some sort of joke. But just a little later, in
the brothel scene, the voice of a compassionate, mature woman
was to be heard. Ronald Bryden movingly describes this
moment:

> Lisa Harrow's Desdemona sees his fear, and tries to gentle it, meet
> it with trust. In one of [director] Barton's most brilliant
> innovations, their fourth act confrontation ('I took you for that
> cunning whore of Venice') is played as a half-naked siesta together,
> the wife softly trying to calm her husband, make him speak, accept

her caresses, and almost succeeding. I've seldom seen acting reach
so near the intimate heart of marriage.

(*Observer*, 12 September 1971)

Her failure to reassure her husband made the willow scene that
shortly followed 'the emotional peak of the evening' (B. A.
Young, *Financial Times*, 10 September 1971), and her death
came close to being another. The production thus reached from
time to time into 'the intimate heart' of the tragedy itself which,
unfortunately, as happens so often, was undercut by an
underplayed Othello and an overplayed Iago.

Maggie Smith's Interpretation, 1964

An 'atmosphere of the most potent sensuality' (Bamber
Gascoigne, quoted in Tynan, p. 107) was Maggie Smith's
contribution to the part several years earlier opposite Laurence
Olivier, in John Dexter's National Theatre production. Smith's
Desdemona countered Olivier's proud, strong-willed, and
highly sexed Othello with a pride, strong will, and sexual
passion of her own. Here, in modern times, was the fairest
warrior of them all. The strength of her many-sided characterisation gave depth and meaning to Othello's tragedy, and
may be one reason that Olivier's consciously developed
'realistic' interpretation turned out to be, in the end, more
'romantic' than he and director John Dexter had intended. For
once, the mutual attraction of Othello and Desdemona was both
plausible and convincing. Throughout the play, Smith made
evident the power that her Desdemona had over Othello, as at
the beginning of the temptation scene when she never let him
take his eyes off her while she pleaded the case for Cassio.
Olivier, self-assured and 'egotistical' as Othello, was nevertheless completely at her mercy, almost shrivelling in weakness
when he responded that he could deny her nothing.

Bernard Levin has written that, in the final scene, Olivier's
Othello 'kills with such sorrow that it is unbearable; he dies
with such consciousness of waste that it is more unbearable yet'
(quoted in Tynan, p. 103). Smith's Desdemona, most critics
found, made credible that 'sorrow' and 'consciousness of
waste'. And where Desdemona is strong and believable, Iago is

diminished. At the beginning of the fourth act, Othello and
Iago (Olivier and Finlay) enter together; and, as the ensign
inflames the general's imagination with a verbal picture of
Desdemona 'naked with her friend in bed / An hour or more',
'the two men even begin to sway gently from side to side, locked
together in the rhythm of Othello's pain' (Tynan, p. 10). But
the most memorable moment of this production counters this
appalling scene – when Othello lifts the slain Desdemona from
her deathbed and rocks back and forth with her locked in his
arms. Othello's tragedy, not Iago's triumph, is what comes
through, as well as Othello's triumph over Iago in that his
original faith in Desdemona was warranted all along.

A few critics found Smith's Desdemona 'no more than
adequate' or too much like 'an animated talking doll'. The
dramatic critic of *The Times* wrote that she 'is on very distant
terms with the part': 'Obviously a mettlesome girl who would
not for an instant have endured domestic tyranny, she intro-
duces facetious modern inflexions (for instance her giggling
reference to "These Men" in the bedchamber scene [IV iii])
which clash destructively with the character' (22 April 1964).
Reviewing the film made from the stage production, John
Simon remarked that 'Maggie Smith's Desdemona is fine, if
you like the play with two Emilias in it' (*Private Screenings*, 1967,
p. 213). These last two critics were objecting apparently to a
Desdemona not doll-like enough but, rather, like Emilia, a
knowing woman of the world who gives as much as she gets. On
the other hand, the calm dignity that Smith invested her
Desdemona with at the beginning of the play and the stupified
resignation that came over her later, after Othello's violent and
incomprehensible treatment of her, were the emotions not of a
'doll' but of an aristocrat's daughter, whose act of marriage was
as courageous as any of Othello's heroic exploits. There was a
touching moment in the Senate scene when she reached out to
her father to try to make him understand, and then registered
sorrow when she failed. But Smith's Desdemona was immune
from self-pity. Tynan describes her reaction to Othello's
striking her 'across the face with the rolled-up proclamation he
has received from Lodovico' in Act IV, scene i, as 'not the usual
collapse into sobs; it is one of deep shame and embarrassment,

for Othello's sake as well as her own. She is outraged, but tries out of loyalty not to show it' (p. 10).

As a proper Elizabethan wife, Desdemona tells her husband: 'Be as your fancies teach you. / Whate'er you be, I am obedient' [III iii 88–9]. Smith's Desdemona has given up everything for Othello, but she will not relinquish her self-respect or individuality. Admittedly, Smith did not bring to the role one dimension of Desdemona that the text makes clear – the 'sweetness' that Othello sees in her, just as Olivier did not bring to Othello the grandeur and heroic nobility traditionally associated with the part. But, given their approaches, the team of Olivier and Smith meshed together as few Othellos and Desdemonas have in the stage history of the play and at least put the emphasis where it should be: on Othello *and* Desdemona.

10   EPILOGUE

Television 'Othello' or 'The Play of Iago'

The *Othello* most widely seen, ever, was not a stage performance but Jonathan Miller's production for BBC-television, which was first shown in October 1981. Anthony Hopkins played Othello; Bob Hoskins, Iago; and Penelope Wilton, Desdemona.

That many critics thought it should have been retitled *Iago* is not surprising because television is strictly a director's medium, and Iago is a director's dream because he so effortlessly explains away ambivalences of character and reduces the complexities of life to a simple, unified vision of 'benefit and injury'. With the availability of video cassettes for purchase or rental, Miller's television version is likely to have lasting impact and, therefore, deserves separate discussion.

Othello, more totally than any other play by Shakespeare, exploits the very nature of theatre itself, which 'requires us to see, overhear and interpret the simulations of those who try to make us believe that all is true' (T. P. Matheson, *Times Literary Supplement*, 19 November 1982). As witnesses to a live performance, audiences of the play often *see* a multiplicity of happenings and *overhear* shifting points of view simultaneously, and out of this welter of conflicting sights and sounds must *interpret* the evidence before them; no camera directs their attention and tells them what to look for.

The so-called 'encavement scene' [IV i] provides a vivid example in microcosm of how *Othello* operates. In a live performance Iago as playwright and director sets up a situation for Othello 'to see, overhear and interpret' and, from his point of view, does so successfully: Othello interprets what he sees and overhears, Iago and Cassio talking at a distance about Bianca, as 'proof' of Desdemona's infidelity. In a television presentation Iago becomes Othello's 'cinematic eye', which, like the narrow focus of a camera, calls the shots. In the BBC-television rendition of this scene the camera does not permit us to see and overhear the two planes of the play, Iago's *and* Shakespeare's, working simultaneously and in opposition. We watch mainly from Othello's point of view, which is, of course, the one that Iago has engineered. The dialogue between Iago and Cassio as they laugh over Bianca – words so clear in the text – is scarcely audible to both Othello *and* to the television viewer. We see and hear, as it were from behind Othello's back, not from the more spacious viewpoint of a theatre audience. Even Othello's frequent interjections – his 'interpretations' of what he 'sees' and 'overhears' – are for the most part cut, and at times he almost disappears as we inhabit his sensibility. The camera, Othello and the audience are one.

The televised production of *Othello* offers other instances where the camera tells us what to see and, therefore, interprets for us. In the final scene, Desdemona's deathbed, which should dominate our vision, is often out of the picture entirely, even when, perversely, Othello stabs himself and dies 'upon a kiss'. Othello simply falls out of the picture, not onto the bed to kiss Desdemona. But, as he falls through the bottom of the frame or screen, the shot reveals Iago, thereby emphasising his dominant role as instigator of this dastardly deed and now as victor in his 'practical joke'. Miller admits that he finds Iago 'the most interesting character in the play' and he permits the camera to focus on him as often as possible (*The BBC TV Shakespeare 'Othello'*, 1981, p. 25). As Desdemona assures Cassio that she will never give up his 'suit' with 'my lord', Emilia says, 'Madam, here comes my lord' [III iii 29]. But Iago, not his general, enters first and occupies the screen. When Lodovico, speaking to Iago, says of Othello, 'I am sorry that I am deceived in him' [IV i 284], it is Iago's face that peers into the camera. Even where the text is silent on Iago, the production brings him to the fore, as in the play's second scene where he rudely interrupts Brabantio's threats to Othello with his cackling; Brabantio's line [75], 'I'll have't disputed on', is diverted to Iago from Othello, to whom all readers, surely, would direct it. Nowhere, however, are the values of this production more sharply emphasised than at the very end where, instead of allowing the tragedy of Othello to make its fullest impact upon the audience, the camera focuses on the villain as he is being led down a long corridor. Even after he is out of sight, Iago's incessant giggling continues to be heard till the screen fades out. Whether he is overjoyed at what he has wrought, even his own destruction, or, maybe, as one reviewer believed, just gone 'bonkers' (*Daily Telegraph*, 5 October 1981) is almost beside the point. Irreparably lost is the vision of black Othello embracing in death white Desdemona.

Simply as a cinematic experience, the BBC-television *Othello* was always beautiful to look at: night scenes reminiscent of Rembrandt; day scenes, of Vermeer; costumes, of Velazquez and El Greco. Not a barely civilised fortress outpost but a magnificent palace, suggested to Miller by a Renaissance palace in Urbino, is the setting of the Cyprus scenes. But the excluding features of the camera's eye widen further the normal gap in *Othello* studies between criticism and live performance. On the wide, scenery-less Elizabethan stage, words and their accompanying gestures alone determined meaning; words and their accompanying gestures are the sole 'evidence' that Iago offers Othello of his 'honesty', and they are all that Shakespeare offers us for interpretation.

Orson Welles understood the difference between live per-formance and film uniquely, for in his movie version of *Othello* (1951; released 1955) he frankly disavowed reverence for Shakespeare's written text and made visually explicit the

imagery and themes implicit in the poetry. In the Welles film,
the imposing architecture of civilised Venice contrasts sharply
with the forlorn fortress outpost of Cyprus. (The Cyprus scenes
were actually shot in Morocco.) Vast spaces separate characters, literally as well as metaphorically. Darkness overwhelms
light. Iago kills Roderigo in a steaming Turkish bath – a kind of
'cistern for foul toads / To knot and gender in' [IV ii 60–1]. The
'net' that Iago weaves to 'enmesh them all' is reflected in the
many nets, traps, and cages throughout the film, and Iago
himself looks down upon the funeral procession of Othello and
Desdemona, with which the film begins and ends, from a
wooden cage that had been hoisted to the top of the fortress
walls.

Nothing illustrates so well, however, the distorting effect of
the camera as the filmed version (1965) of the 1964 National
Theatre production. The film does not record an actual stage
performance, for the production was moved to a sound studio
for filming, and some changes and cuts were introduced; but
the stage production was not essentially redesigned, so that
what the viewer sees on screen approximates, more or less, a
film recording of the stage performance. On stage Olivier
succeeded in keeping the focus on Othello as the play's central
character, but the film elevated Frank Finlay's Iago into a
prominence that he never enjoyed in live performance. The
close-up shot, much favoured by the camera, is a great leveller;
and the frequent close-ups of Iago in soliloquy, where he
seemed to be inviting the cinema audience to share his crafty
machinations, did much to make Finlay appear more nearly
the equal of Olivier. At the same time the close-ups of Olivier
dangerously heightened, to an uncomfortable degree, the kind
of histrionic exaggeration that made his stage appearance so
compelling.

Television, much more so than the large-scale cinematic
film, particularly favours the close-up shot, possibly because
the smaller screen inevitably, though not necessarily, invites
intimacy and devalues the heroic scale and the space that it
demands. Mark Crispin Miller has pointed out that 'passion
. . . rarely registers on television except as something comical or
suspect': 'The medium therefore undercuts the warrior's ardor'
and 'also strains out the intensity of suffering, flattening the

martyr as it ridicules the persecutor, trivialising both victim and tormentor' (*New Republic*, 29 November 1982). These observations grew out of television's role in spreading anti-war sentiment in the United States during the Vietnam conflict by literally bringing into homes the unglamorous, unheroic aspects of the battlefield, as it might have done had the war in the Falklands continued. They also help to explain why television's small screen accommodates Iago so readily but squanders the magnificence of Othello – which Jonathan Miller claimed not to see anyway: 'What is interesting is that it's not the fall of the great but the disintegration of the ordinary, of the representative character' (*The BBC TV Shakespeare 'Othello'*, p. 23). And they may explain, incidentally, why the only moving performance in the last scene is Emilia's (acted by Rosemary Leach).

As Iago, Bob Hoskins in Miller's production plays 'a practical joker of a peculiarly appalling kind', described by W. H. Auden (in an essay acknowledged by Miller) as one who does not satisfy 'any concrete desire of his nature' but exists to demonstrate 'the weakness of others' ('The Joker in the Pack', in *The Dyer's Hand and Other Essays*, 1968, pp. 253, 256). To be sure, the television production does emphasise class distinctions. With his cockney accent, cropped hair, simple black leather costume, and the snakelike manner in which he sidles up to the courtiers, Iago, not Othello, is the outsider among the well-spoken, handsomely coiffed, and elegantly attired Venetians. Class hatred alone, however, or deep envy of the 'daily beauty' of others does not fully explain this Iago, whom Hoskins himself refers to as 'one nasty bastard', who 'gets his kicks from causing pain'. Miller refers to his 'mischievous gangster's merriment', not unlike Hoskins's portrayal of the cruelly mischievous gangster, Harold Shand, in the movie *The Long Good Friday*. In the opening scene of *Othello*, Hoskins cups in his hands water from a fountain and sprays Brabantio with it, as if to indicate his obvious enjoyment of mischief for its own sake. No deep passion or emotion troubles him. When Desdemona turns to him for comfort [IV ii], he treats her like a child, making silly noises and faces, and after she exits bursts into laughter. When, in the next to the last scene, the net enmeshing others begins to appear as if it might enmesh him

also, this Iago shows not the slightest sign of desperation but
follow his proclamation, 'This is the night / That either makes
me, or fordoes me quite', with the heartiest of laughs.

The frequent close-ups of a constantly laughing Iago had the
effect of overfamiliarising him and thus making him appear less
fearsome with each appearance. The 'merry gangster' interpretation also made Anthony Hopkins's Othello seem too
gullible or too easily victimised to be authentically tragic.
Understanding only too well television's power to dilute the
heroic, Jonathan Miller and Hopkins opted for a low-key
Othello, subdued and quietly confident as the play opens, but
not romantically heroic or soldierly. Instead of the traditionally
impressive entrance, Othello's first appearance on screen
shows him busily fussing with his ensign's gorget, again
deflecting more attention onto Iago. In sharp contrast to
Olivier, Hopkins eschewed heavy make-up, just darkening his
skin ever so slightly that at times he appeared almost literally
'more fair', as the Duke says [I iii 287], than the Venetian
grandees around him. Miller told an interviewer that he did
'not see the play as being about color, but as being about
jealousy – which is something we are all vulnerable to' (*Women's
Wear Daily*, 22 June 1981). An emphasis on racism as we
understand that term today clearly demeans the play, but at
the same time to deny the undeniable references in the text to
Othello's blackness and its symbolic value and to focus on so
narrow a theme as an ordinary man's jealousy provoked by an
envious 'practical joker' comes perilously close to invalidating
the play as tragedy. Because of this narrow view, some
reviewers felt that Hopkins's Othello had no 'centre' to it.

If the medium, as Hopkins and Miller saw it, did not allow
for overplaying, except to emphasise Othello's mad fits after
the temptation scene, underplaying brought at times its own
rewards. Rather than attempting to convey the heroic majesty
of a Robeson, the sexual passion of an Olivier, the gentle
romanticism of a Mason, or the vulnerability of a Jones,
Hopkins gave us an introverted Othello. One of the most
deeply touching moments of the television production occurs at
the beginning of the temptation scene when, still in very good
humour as Desdemona exits, he says:

> Excellent wretch! Perdition catch my soul
> But I do love thee! And when I love thee not,
> Chaos is come again.   [iii iii 90–2]

Most Othellos deliver these lines somewhat light-heartedly as if
they could never possibly believe that chaos might come again,
but the television close-up of Hopkins's face works very
effectively here: he registers no suspicion of Desdemona at this
point, but his penetrating stare and haunted expression,
coupled with his subdued delivery, make one believe that this is
the face of a man who really knows what chaos is all about and
is deeply fearful of its return. In Desdemona this Othello's
heart has found refuge. Hopkins delivers the great Senate
speech not as a discovery of love, as the structure of the play
demands, but as 'a game in which he wearily consents to amuse
his colleagues' (Peter Conrad's review of the production, *Times
Literary Supplement*, 16 October 1981). His quiet delivery of
Othello's final speech conveys a tragic sense of what he had lost
and effectively restores him to dignity. But the BBC-television
production, with Iago as its dominant figure, allowed this
Othello to be only fitfully moving.

   The one genuine triumph of the televised *Othello* – the critics
are almost unanimous – was Penelope Wilton's Desdemona.
Hers was by far the best rendering of the Shakespearean verse
rhythms; Hopkins tended to invoke distracting emphases and
pauses, and Hoskins lost the rhythm entirely in his cockney
rendition. A truly spirited heroine, Wilton's Desdemona made
one understand why Othello should have wanted 'to be free
and bounteous to her mind' [i iii 262]. At her first appearance,
in the Senate, she looks at Othello so lovingly that it becomes
apparent at once what this marriage means to her. As her
relationship with Othello continues to break down, however,
she never ceases to fight for her personal integrity: 'By heaven,
you do me wrong', she defiantly shouts at him after he has
called her 'impudent strumpet' [iv ii 80]. To the bedchamber or
willow scene [iv iii], beautifully composed to contrast the
idealism of Desdemona seated near a lighted candle and the
pragmatism of Emilia seated near a skull, Wilton adds genuine
depth as she 'tunelessly [hums] the Willow Song under her
breath, too aggrieved for the palliation of music' (Conrad). In

the final scene, she bravely fights for her life; but, unfortunately, in her last moments the camera too often focuses away
from her face. Her final words, so controversial in criticism and
so much a key to her character, are barely comprehensible.
Could Othello, standing off at a distance, possibly have heard
them? And after her death the camera keeps cutting away from
'the tragic loading of this bed' to reduce or even deny the full
impact of her death on Othello – and on us.

In keeping with Miller's feeling about the 'domestic' quality
of this particular Shakespearean tragedy, most of the action is
confined to interior scenes. The storm that begins Act II is
greatly subdued; the reunion of the storm-tossed survivors
takes place not at the port but in the great hall of the palace.
Unlike Welles's film with its greatly expanded sense of
foreboding space, Miller's television production avoids suggestions of a larger world. Instead, even amidst the splendour of
the scenes, shades of the prisonhouse keep closing in. Not
heroic or romantic tragedy but, as the *Times Literary Supplement*
headlined its review, 'Living-room tragedy'.

READING LIST

The edition used throughout is that by Kenneth Muir (New Penguin Shakespeare, 1968). The editions by M. R. Ridley (New Arden, 1958) and Alice Walker & J. Dover Wilson (New Cambridge, 1957) have heavily annotated texts and much material about themes, characterisation, textual problems and stage history. The New Variorum edition by H. H. Furness (2nd edn, 1886) is useful for its compilation of earlier English and Continental criticism (including Macaulay's comments in the *Edinburgh Review*). Lawrence J. Ross's edition of the play (1974) has an extensive bibliography. The most readily useful bibliographical work is Robert Hapgood's contribution on the play in Stanley Wells (ed.), *Shakespeare: Select Bibliographical Guides* (1973). Useful supplementary bibliographies are those by Ronald Berman, *A Reader's Guide to Shakespeare* (1965, pp. 102–7) and S. A. Tannenbaum, *Shakespeare's 'Othello': A Concise Bibliography* (1943).

Geoffrey Bullough's *Narrative and Dramatic Sources of Shakespeare*, vol. 7 (1975), contains translations of Cinthio and other possible sources. Shakespeare's transformation of Cinthio's narrative into drama is examined in Max Bluestone's *From Story to Stage* (1974).

John Wain's *Othello* in the Macmillan Casebook series (1971) includes generous critical selections from Thomas Rymer, Samuel Johnson, Coleridge, Bradley, T. S. Eliot, Wilson Knight, Empson, Leavis, Helen Gardner, John Bayley, Auden and Neville Coghill. The play text, a selection of criticism and a translation of Cinthio make up Leonard F. Dean's *A Casebook on Othello* (1961).

Shakespeare Survey 21 (1968), devoted mainly to *Othello*, has articles on its time-sequence, relationship to comedy, historical background, structure and themes – all prefaced by Helen Gardner's essay, '*Othello*: A Retrospect, 1900–67', pp. 1–11, in which she notes that the play's characters 'come as physical realities not wholly amenable to intellectual analysis'.

Actors' responses to the play are quoted and discussed in Marvin Rosenberg, *The Masks of Othello* (1961) and Carol Jones Carlisle, *Shakespeare from the Greenroom* (1969). Daniel Seltzer takes us back to the first production in 'Elizabethan Acting in *Othello*', *Shakespeare*

Quarterly, 10 (1959), pp. 201–10. The text with full line-by-line commentary on how different actors have responded is given in John Russell Brown's Harbrace Theatre Edition (1973); and Kenneth Tynan's *'Othello' by William Shakespeare: The National Theatre Production* (1966) indicates, scene by scene, the approach by director and cast during rehearsals. Tynan's book also has many photographs and a survey of reviews. Jack J. Jorgens, *Shakespeare on Film* (1977), discusses in detail Orson Welles's film of 1951/1955 and that by Stuart Burges (1965) of the National Theatre production of 1964. A major assessment of the Burges film as a 'great *Othello*' is given by James E. Fisher in 'Olivier and the Realistic *Othello*', *Literature/Film Quarterly*, I (1973), pp. 321–9.

G. K. Hunter's British Academy Lecture of 1967, 'Othello and Colour Prejudice' (reprinted with revisions in his *Dramatic Identities and Cultural Tradition* [1978], pp. 31–59) observes how Shakespeare inverts 'the expected racial values' of his audience. Ruth Cowhig, in 'Actors, Black and Tawny, in the role of Othello – and their Critics', *Theatre Research International*, n.s. 4 (1979), pp. 133–46, shows how actors over the centuries have approached this subject.

The 'inadequacy of language as a substitute for complex reality', as one of the major problems confronted in the play, is discussed in Lawrence Danson's *The Tragic Alphabet* (1974). Susan Snyder – in *The Comic Matrix of Shakespeare's Tragedies* (1979) – is concerned with the relationship of the play to the comedies. Some cogent thoughts on the subject are offered in Carol Thomas Neely's 'Women and Men in *Othello* . . .', *Shakespeare Studies*, 10 (1977), pp. 133–58. Neely sees the play as 'a terrifying completion of the comedies'.

In *The Story of the Night* (1961) John Holloway offers a detailed analysis of the temptation episode [III iii] which effectively answers Leavis's criticism that Othello is too easily jealous. Barbara Everett – 'Reflections on the Sentimentalist's Othello', *Critical Quarterly*, 3 (1961), pp. 127–39 – notes that Othello's, not Iago's, view of Desdemona is the 'realistic' one. John Bayley discusses the 'structure of love' in *Shakespeare and Tragedy* (1981); and Arthur Kirsch offers a psychological perspective in *Shakespeare and the Experience of Love* (1981). Of full-length treatments of the play in recent years, notable is Jane Adamson, *'Othello' as Tragedy* (1980), which treats it as a tragedy of the failing attempts people make 'to escape from real or imagined pain'.

The importance of structural considerations is explained in Moody Prior's 'Character in Relation to Action in *Othello*', *Modern Philology*, 44 (1947), pp. 225–37. Alvin Kernan discusses the 'symbolic geography' of Venice and Cyprus in his Introduction to the Signet edition (1963).

INDEX OF NAMES

Aldridge, Ira 46
American Shakespeare Theatre 42 *passim*
Auden, W. H., 'The Joker in the Pack' 77

Barton, John 42, 53, 63, 70
BBC TV Shakespeare 'Othello' 75, 77
BIANCA 17, 18, 19, 22, 30, 74
Booth, Edwin 57
BRABANTIO 16 *passim*
Bradley, A. C., *Shakespearean Tragedy* 10
Brown, John Russell, *Shakespeare's 'Othello': The Harbrace Theatre Edition* 12
Brustein, Robert 64, 69
Bryden, Ronald 44, 53, 63, 70-1
Bullough, Geoffrey, *Narrative and Dramatic Sources of Shakespeare* 13

CASSIO: compared to Cinthio's Corporal 17-18; cashiering of 20, 28; as governor of Cyprus 35-6
Cinthio, Giraldi, *Gli Hecatommithi* 13-20 *passim*
Clurman, Harold, *The Naked Image* 47, 62
Coe, Peter 42
Commedia dell'arte 27

Danson, Lawrence, *The Tragic Alphabet* 41
DESDEMONA: compared to Cinthio's Disdemona 15-16; last words 34; inspiration for Othello's 'Farewell' speech 41; modern performances 66-73
Dexter, John 42, 48, 59, 61, 71

Eliot, T. S., 'Shakespeare and the Stoicism of Seneca' 29-30, 32
Elizabeth I 47
EMILIA: and handkerchief 19; friendship with Desdemona 22; as 'voice of reality' 29; television (Rosemary Leach) 77

Ferrer, Jose 42, 58-9, 60, 64-5, 67; 'The Role of Iago in Shakespeare's *Othello*' 58
Finlay, Frank 42, 59-62, 64, 72, 76
Forster, E. M., *Howards End* 51

Gardner, Helen 26; 'The Noble Moor' 10
Gaskill, William 56
Gibson, William, *Shakespeare's Game* 41
Gielgud, John 44, 51

Hagen, Uta 42, 67-8
Harbage, Alfred, *As They Liked It* 15
Harrow, Lisa 42, 69-71
Hart, Cecilia 42, 69
Hopkins, Anthony 42, 73, 78-9
Hoskins, Bob 42, 73, 77-8, 79

IAGO: as centre of interest 11; compared to Cinthio's Ensign 16-17; as invoking the storm of Act II, scene i 21; as playwright-within-the-play 30-2; his silence at the end 35; his 'little music' 36; dialogue with Roderigo and soliloquy at end of Act I 37-9, 40; his name 47; modern performances 57-66; as director's dream 73; as 'practical joker' 77

Jacobi, Derek 61
James, Emrys 42, 44, 62-3, 64, 65
James, Henry, *The Scenic Art* 57
Jones, James Earl 42, 43, 46, 55-7, 62, 63, 64, 68-9, 78
Jonson, Ben: 'humours' husbands in 26

Kean, Edmund: as 'tawny' or 'white' Moor 47
Knight, G. Wilson, *The Wheel of Fire* 36

Leach, Rosemary 77
Leavis, F. R., 'Diabolic Intellect and the Noble Hero' 10, 48, 49, 51-2, 60, 62
Levin, Harry, *Shakespeare and the Revolution of the Times* 47

84

Macaulay, Thomas Babington 9
MacLiammóir, Micheál 43
McCarthy, Mary, *Sights and Spectacles* 58
Mason, Brewster 42, 43, 44, 52–5, 56, 57, 58, 62, 63, 69–70, 78
Matheson, T. P. 74
Miller, Jonathan 42, 73–80 *passim*
Miller, Mark Crispin 76–7
Molière: 'humours' husbands in 26

National Theatre 42 *passim*
Neely, Carol Thomas, 'Women and Men in *Othello*' 22

Olivier (ed. Logan Gourlay) 56
Olivier, Laurence 42, 43, 45, 47, 48–52, 53, 54, 55, 56–7, 59, 60, 62, 71, 72, 73, 76, 78; *Confessions of an Actor* 50
Othello: textual problems, relations to Cinthio 18–19; Quarto, First Folio act divisions 20–1; relationship to comedies 25–7; staging 43–5; modern racial concerns 47–8; theatricality 73–4
OTHELLO: paradox of character 9–10; main problem of interpretation 10–11, 20, 29, 43; temptation scene [III iii] 12–13 *passim*; sympathy for 19–20; as romance or epic figure 27; Senate speech 32–3; and handkerchief 33–4; final speech 34–5; 'Othello music' 36, 40, 52; 'Farewell' speech 40–1; modern performances 45–57; performances by black or white actors 47–8; relationship with Desdemona 66–7

Plummer, Christopher 42, 62, 63–6

Redgrave, Michael 51
Robeson, Paul 42, 43, 45, 46–7, 48, 49, 54, 55, 57, 60, 62, 64, 67, 70, 78
Roderigo 16, 22; dialogue with Iago 37–9, 40
Rosenberg, Marvin, *The Masks of Othello* 59
Royal Shakespeare Company 42, 44–5 *passim*
Rymer, Thomas, *A Short View of Tragedy* 14, 19, 23, 25, 33

Salvini, Tommaso 51, 57
Shakespeare, William: Aaron (*Titus Andronicus*) 27; Hamlet 11; Lear 11, 32; Macbeth 11; *Troilus and Cressida* 26; possible revisions of *Othello* 18–19; taking risks with structure 25; comparison with Iago as playwrights 30
Simon, John 68; *Private Screenings* 50, 72
Smith, Maggie 42, 71–3

Tynan, Kenneth (ed.), '*Othello*' by William Shakespeare 48, 50, 51, 61, 71, 72–3

Webster, Margaret 42, 43, 45, 46, 58—9, 67—8: *Shakespeare without Tears* 36
Welles, Orson 43, 75–6, 80
Wiest, Dianne 42, 68–9, 70
Wilson, John Dover, the Cambridge *Othello* 46–7
Wilton, Penelope 42, 73, 79–80

Yeats, W. B., 'Lapis Lazuli' 10–11, 29

Zeffirelli, Franco 44

FOR READER'S NOTES

FOR READER'S NOTES

FOR READER'S NOTES

FOR READER'S NOTES